Mirror, Mirror:
Rethinking a generation

What
does
your
mirror
say
about
you?

Niharika Singh

INDIA · SINGAPORE · MALAYSIA

ISBN
Paperback 979-8-89632-769-1
Hardcase 979-8-89673-713-1

Contents

Preface

We are a generation caught between extremes—striving for success, yet suffocated by superficial definitions of happiness, beauty, and achievement. In a world dominated by social media, influencer culture, and the commodification of personal identity, we are more connected than ever, yet increasingly disconnected from ourselves and each other. *Mirror Mirror: Rethinking a Generation* is an exploration of the contradictions that define our time.

This book is born from a deep desire to question the prevailing narratives that dictate how we should think, live, and feel. I have long observed how the pursuit of an idealized image—whether it be the perfect social persona, the elusive notion of "wokeness," or the relentless search for validation—has led to a sense of emptiness in many of us. In our pursuit of being seen, we have lost sight of who we truly are.

Through these pages, I aim to unravel the complexities of the modern age, from the flaws of "woke" culture to the intoxicating allure of escapism, all while reflecting on the deeper cost of conforming to societal expectations. This book is not an attack on progress or empowerment, but a call to embrace a more thoughtful, intentional approach to personal and collective growth.

I believe in the power of modesty—not as a restriction, but as a means of finding clarity in a world that often drowns out our true voices. By re-evaluating our values and challenging the false promises of instant gratification, we can reclaim authenticity and build a generation that prioritizes well-being over empty aspirations.

This book is not just a critique; it is a manifesto for change. It is an invitation to step away from the distractions that keep us stuck and to embark on a journey of self-awareness, genuine connection, and lasting fulfilment. As we examine the roots of modern struggles, we will explore practical solutions that can help us break free from the cycles of confusion and disillusionment.

If you, too, are looking for a way to rethink the status quo and create a life that is both meaningful and mindful, this book is for you. It is time for us to look into the mirror—not to see an image we have been told to aspire to, but to see ourselves clearly, without distortion.

Chapter 1

The Illusion of Perfection

A Childhood Apart

Growing up, I always felt a step out of sync with the world around me. While my friends found joy in the newest toys, trendy clothes, or the latest tech gadgets, I couldn't shake the feeling that there was more to life than keeping up with the latest "must-have." This mindset wasn't easy to maintain, especially as I became more aware of how starkly it contrasted with those around me.

I often felt left out—not because I lacked material possessions, but because I couldn't embrace the same value system. It wasn't that I didn't appreciate beautiful things; I did. But I struggled to understand why they seemed to hold so much power over how people saw themselves and each other. Over time, this mindset put me at odds with many of my peers. Disagreements bubbled up, sometimes over something as trivial as my refusal to buy into the latest trend, other times over deeper philosophical differences about what truly mattered.

Over time, this mindset put me at odds with many of my peers. Disagreements bubbled up, sometimes over something as trivial as my refusal to buy into the latest trend, other times over deeper philosophical differences about what truly mattered. These experiences shaped me, planting the seeds of this chapter. They made me acutely aware of the heavy toll materialism takes—not just on our wallets, but on our souls.

Perfectionism isn't just a personal trait; it's a societal demand in disguise. As we strive to meet unrelenting standards, we rarely pause to question who sets these benchmarks.

Advertisers promise us flawless skin, ideal bodies, and impeccable lifestyles, while algorithms ensure that the ideal remains tantalizingly out of reach. In this endless pursuit, we lose more than money—we lose peace of mind.

For instance, studies have shown that perfectionism correlates with increased levels of anxiety, depression, and burnout. Yet, these psychological tolls are rarely discussed in the glossy, curated images we consume daily. The polished veneer hides sleepless nights, strained relationships, and crippling self-doubt.

This societal obsession with perfection has also warped our perception of success. We're conditioned to celebrate achievements without acknowledging the sacrifices behind them. We laud the entrepreneur who "hustled" their way to wealth, but not the toll it took on their health or personal relationships. The illusion persists because we rarely see the full story.

The Seduction of Materialism

Materialism is not a new phenomenon, but in this digital age, it has evolved into something far more pervasive. Advertisements are no longer confined to billboards or magazine pages; they now live in our pockets, constantly vying for our attention through curated feeds and influencer endorsements.

The allure of materialism lies in its promise: if you own this, you will be happy. If you wear that, you will be admired. If you buy into this, you will belong. But this promise is hollow, a mirage that vanishes the moment you draw near.

Materialism, at its core, is the belief that acquiring possessions brings happiness and fulfilment. While this isn't a new concept—humans have long sought comfort in ownership—it has taken on a new form in the digital age. Social media platforms, fuelled by algorithms designed to maximise engagement, have amplified materialism to unprecedented levels.

The 20th century saw the rise of consumer culture, spurred by industrialisation and mass production. But the 21st century transformed this culture into something more insidious. Now, advertisements don't just sell products; they sell lifestyles, identities, and aspirations. Every scroll through Instagram or TikTok is a curated showcase of the "good life," where luxury and exclusivity are the ultimate goals.

Fear of missing out (FOMO) isn't a new phenomenon, but it has become weaponized in the digital age. Social media platforms capitalize on our natural fear of exclusion by presenting an endless parade of experiences we feel compelled to chase. From exclusive vacations to limited-edition products, FOMO drives consumer behaviour and deepens the cycle of dissatisfaction.

Take the rise of "drop culture," where brands release products in small batches, creating artificial scarcity. This tactic turns shopping into a competitive sport, where acquiring the latest item feels like a personal victory. But the satisfaction is fleeting, replaced by the pressure to keep up with the next trend.

FOMO extends beyond material possessions; it influences how we spend our time. We attend events we're not interested in, take photos to prove we were there, and curate online personas that reflect an idealized version of our lives. The result? A generation that feels more connected than ever but is increasingly lonely and unfulfilled.

This pervasive messaging leaves little room for self-reflection. The idea that happiness can be bought has become so deeply ingrained that questioning it feels almost heretical.

Yet, as research consistently shows, material possessions rarely deliver the lasting happiness they promise. Instead, they create a cycle of desire and dissatisfaction, leaving people trapped in an endless pursuit of more.

The social media Marketplace

Platforms like Instagram and TikTok have transformed materialism into a performance art. Influencers flaunt designer handbags, luxury vacations, and picture-perfect homes, creating a culture where success is measured not by character or contribution but by possessions. The subtle—and sometimes not-so-subtle—message is clear: if you don't have these things, you're not enough.

This has created a toxic cycle of comparison. People see these images and feel compelled to keep up, often stretching their finances and compromising their authenticity in the process. The pressure is immense, and the consequences are real: mounting debt, mental health struggles, and a pervasive sense of inadequacy.

The Cost of Conformity

One of the most insidious effects of materialism is its ability to erase individuality. In a world where everyone is chasing the same branded dream, there's little room for uniqueness. Trends dictate not just what we wear but also how we think and what we value.

This loss of individuality isn't just a personal tragedy—it's a societal one. Creativity, innovation, and progress thrive on diversity of thought and expression. When we all follow the same script, we lose the richness that makes life meaningful.

The Physical Appeal Trap

Another layer of this illusion is the obsession with physical appearance. Social media, once a tool for connection, has become a mirror in which we endlessly scrutinise ourselves. Filters and photo-editing apps have created an unattainable standard of beauty, and millions strive to meet it, often at great emotional and physical cost.

The Mask of Filters

Filters don't just smooth skin or whiten teeth—they erase individuality. They create a homogenised version of beauty that is both alluring and deeply damaging. By presenting a flawless facade, filters reinforce the idea that imperfections are flaws to be corrected rather than unique traits to be celebrated.

For many, the result is a profound sense of dissatisfaction with their natural selves. The more we compare ourselves to these filtered images, the more we feel like we fall short. And so, begins a cycle of self-criticism and striving for a perfection that doesn't exist.

The Disconnect from Self-Awareness

Materialism and the obsession with appearances both contribute to a growing lack of self-awareness. When our lives revolve around external validation—whether it's through possessions or physical appeal—we lose touch with our inner selves.

Living for Likes

The pursuit of likes and followers has turned self-expression into a performance. Instead of sharing who we truly are, we curate a version of ourselves that we think will be admired.

This creates a disconnect between our public persona and our private reality, leaving us feeling hollow and unfulfilled.

The Role of Introspection

True self-awareness requires time and space for introspection. It means asking tough questions: *What do I value? What brings me joy? What defines my worth?* But in a world that moves at breakneck speed, where every moment is filled with scrolling or swiping, finding that time and space has become increasingly difficult.

The Psychological Impacts of Materialism and Appearance Obsession

To escape the illusion of perfection, we must embrace authenticity. This requires a shift in mindset: from valuing appearances to valuing experiences, relationships, and personal growth. Authenticity isn't about rejecting ambition or abandoning effort; it's about aligning our actions with our values.

Materialism and the obsession with physical appeal don't just change our outward behaviours—they fundamentally affect how we think and feel.

1. Anxiety and Insecurity

Constant comparison is a thief of joy. Social media exposes us to a curated version of others' lives, making us feel inadequate in comparison. We begin to question: *Why don't I look like that? Why isn't my life as exciting?*

These questions chip away at our confidence, fuelling anxiety and a persistent sense of not being enough. Studies have shown that heavy social media users report higher levels of anxiety, often linked to the fear of missing out (FOMO) and the pressure to keep up appearances.

2. Depression and Loneliness

Ironically, the very platforms designed to connect us can leave us feeling more isolated. When we measure our worth by likes, followers, or comments, our sense of self becomes tied to external validation. If that validation doesn't come—or if it's less than expected—it can lead to feelings of rejection and sadness.

Materialism exacerbates this. When we equate happiness with possessions, we set ourselves up for disappointment. Research has consistently shown that materialistic individuals are less satisfied with their lives and more likely to experience depression.

3. Loss of Authenticity

The pressure to conform to societal standards can erode our authenticity. We hide parts of ourselves that don't align with the "ideal" image, creating a disconnect between who we are and who we pretend to be. This disconnect can lead to feelings of emptiness and a lack of purpose.

4. Burnout

Maintaining a facade is exhausting. Whether it's spending hours curating a perfect Instagram post or working overtime to afford the latest trends, the energy required to keep up with materialistic demands often leads to burnout. This is particularly true for young people juggling social expectations with academic or professional responsibilities.

5. Body Image Issues

Filters and photo-editing apps have distorted our perception of beauty, setting unattainable standards that fuel body dissatisfaction. The desire to look a certain way often leads to harmful behaviours, from extreme dieting to cosmetic procedures. The psychological toll can be devastating, manifesting in low self-esteem, eating disorders, and self-harm.

The Dopamine Loop

Social media platforms are designed to exploit our brain's reward system. Each like, comment, or share triggers a release of dopamine, the "feel-good" chemical. This creates a cycle of reward and craving, compelling users to seek validation through increasingly curated and materialistic posts. Over time, this loop can lead to dependency, making it difficult to separate self-worth from social media metrics.

Financial Stress and Its Consequences

The drive to keep up with materialistic standards often leads to financial strain. For many, the desire to own luxury items results in mounting credit card debt or loans. This financial stress doesn't exist in isolation—it seeps into mental health, relationships, and overall well-being.

Cultural and Generational Impacts

While materialism is often associated with Western consumer culture, its effects are increasingly global. In countries like India and China, rapid economic growth has fuelled a shift towards materialistic values. Traditional markers of success, such as education or community respect, are being overshadowed by the allure of branded lifestyles.

At the same time, younger generations face unique pressures. Gen Z, in particular, navigates a world where digital personas often overshadow real-world identities. The line between aspiration and reality blurs, creating a sense of perpetual inadequacy.

Rediscovering Self-Worth

So how do we combat these psychological effects and reclaim our sense of self-worth? It begins with a shift in perspective.

1. Value Experiences Over Possessions

True happiness comes not from what we own but from what we experience. Prioritise meaningful experiences—time spent with loved ones, moments of personal growth, or opportunities to give back to others.

2. Practice Gratitude

Gratitude is a powerful antidote to materialism. By focusing on what we already have, we can shift our mindset from one of lack to one of abundance.

3. Foster Real Connections

Social media connections are no substitute for real-life relationships. Invest in friendships and communities that uplift and support you.

4. Embrace Imperfections

Recognise that perfection is an illusion. Celebrate your quirks and flaws—they are what make you unique.

5. Seek Professional Help if Needed

If the psychological toll feels overwhelming, don't hesitate to seek help. Therapy can provide tools and strategies for coping with anxiety, depression, and other challenges.

Breaking Free: Reclaiming Individuality and Purpose

So how do we break free from this illusion? How do we reclaim our individuality, our self-worth, and our sense of purpose?

1. Embrace Imperfection

The first step is to recognise that perfection is an illusion. Celebrate your quirks and flaws—they are what make you unique.

2. Redefine Success

Shift your focus from external markers of success to internal ones. Instead of asking, *what do I own?* ask, *What have I contributed?* Instead of chasing status, chase fulfilment.

3. Limit Exposure to Toxic Influences

Be mindful of the content you consume. Unfollow accounts that make you feel inadequate and seek out those that inspire authenticity and positivity.

4. Invest in Real Connections

Spend less time scrolling and more time connecting with the people who matter. Prioritise relationships that uplift and challenge you to grow.

5. Practice Gratitude

Materialism thrives on dissatisfaction. Combat it by focusing on what you already have rather than what you lack. Gratitude is a powerful antidote to the endless cycle of wanting more.

Closing Thoughts

As I reflect on my own experiences, I realise that the feeling of being "left out" wasn't a curse—it was a blessing in disguise. It allowed me to see the cracks in the illusion of perfection and to seek a deeper, more meaningful way of living.

I hope this chapter serves as a wake-up call for those who feel trapped in this cycle. Perfection is not the goal. Authenticity, connection, and purpose are. Let's put down the masks and filters, step off the hamster wheel of materialism, and start living for something real.

Chapter 2

Faith in the Fog

The Rise of Atheism and Agnosticism Among Gen Z: A Trend or a Thoughtful Exploration?

In recent years, a noticeable shift has taken place among younger generations, particularly Gen Z, in how they approach spirituality and religion. A growing number of young people identify as atheist or agnostic. While this might suggest a move toward rational thought and a rejection of traditional belief systems, the motivations behind this shift are often more complex—and sometimes less grounded—than they appear. Many of these individuals arrive at their beliefs not through deep, philosophical examination of existence but through trends, social influences, or a sense of rebellion against institutional structures. This movement calls for introspection on how we shape personal belief systems and highlights the importance of grounding ourselves in a solid sense of purpose, whether spiritual or otherwise.

This transformation isn't occurring in isolation; it reflects broader societal and cultural changes. With increased access to diverse ideas and information, younger generations have been exposed to new frameworks for understanding existence. At the same time, this openness comes with its challenges. The rejection of traditional religion may offer a sense of freedom, but it also raises the question: what replaces it? The rise of atheism and agnosticism is as much about dissatisfaction with existing systems as it is about searching for alternatives.

Historically, shifts in religious or spiritual beliefs have often followed major societal upheavals. For Gen Z, these upheavals include climate anxiety, political instability, and rapid technological advancements. These forces push young people to question long-standing institutions, including religion. However, this questioning often happens in an environment saturated with shallow interpretations and social pressures, making it harder to engage in a meaningful search for truth.

In the 21st century, faith is no longer confined to religious institutions or doctrines. It has splintered into a kaleidoscope of personal beliefs, spiritual practices, and secular philosophies. This diversification reflects humanity's search for meaning in an increasingly complex world, but it also reveals our struggle to find a cohesive narrative.

For Gen Z, this fragmentation is both liberating and overwhelming. The internet has made knowledge about various belief systems readily available, but it has also created an environment where superficial engagement is common. Many young people identify as "spiritual but not religious," blending practices like meditation, astrology, and mindfulness into their lives. While this eclectic approach offers freedom, it can lack the depth and community that organized religion once provided.

Moreover, this trend reflects a deeper hunger for authenticity. In a world dominated by curated online personas and performative beliefs, young people increasingly seek ideas and systems that feel real and relevant. While atheism and agnosticism may provide a sense of clarity for some, for others, it may be a way to signal belonging in a society that prizes individuality and independence.

In examining this shift, it is essential to avoid painting it in black and white terms. This movement is neither wholly shallow nor wholly profound; rather, it exists on a spectrum. By exploring the nuances of this trend, we can better understand how young people are navigating one of life's most challenging questions: what does it mean to believe?

Major cultural and societal shifts have historically influenced spiritual beliefs, and Gen Z is no exception. Events like the COVID-19 pandemic, climate change, and political unrest have led to a collective questioning of traditional institutions, including religion.

The pandemic, in particular, forced many to confront their mortality and the fragility of life. For some, this led to a renewal of faith, while for others, it prompted a rejection of religious dogma in favour of existential exploration. The climate crisis has also inspired eco-spirituality movements, where environmental stewardship is viewed as a moral imperative tied to spiritual well-being.

Atheism and Agnosticism in the Digital Age

For Gen Z, the digital age has played a massive role in shaping beliefs and attitudes. Social media platforms, where people share opinions freely and engage in open debates, have become major battlegrounds for discussions on religion, spirituality, and existence. It's not uncommon for users to post memes or videos mocking religious figures or promoting agnostic ideologies, often with little exploration of the deeper implications of these beliefs. In this environment, atheism and agnosticism may appear as easy alternatives to the doctrines of organised religion, offering freedom from what many see as restrictive ideologies.

Social media has also amplified the visibility of atheistic and agnostic voices, making these perspectives more accessible than ever. Influencers, content creators, and public intellectuals have taken to platforms like YouTube and TikTok to share their critiques of religion. While some provide thoughtful analysis, others rely on provocative, attention-grabbing tactics that oversimplify complex ideas. For young viewers, this creates a skewed perception of what it means to reject religion, turning atheism or agnosticism into a trendy identity rather than a deeply considered stance.

In a world where traditional sources of meaning are being questioned, many young people are turning inward. Practices like journaling, therapy, and mindfulness have gained popularity as tools for self-discovery. However, this inward focus can sometimes lead to isolation, as the communal aspects of traditional religion are replaced by individualistic pursuits.

The search for purpose often intersects with activism. For Gen Z, fighting for social justice or environmental causes can serve as a form of spiritual expression. This alignment of values and actions offers a sense of purpose, but it can also lead to burnout if not balanced with self-care and reflection.

Additionally, the algorithmic nature of social media often reinforces echo chambers. Users who engage with atheist or agnostic content are more likely to be exposed to similar material, further entrenching their beliefs. This digital reinforcement can make it challenging to encounter alternative perspectives or critically examine one's own views. Unlike philosophical discussions of the past, which required effort and study, the digital age offers quick, surface-level engagement with profound ideas, potentially leading to a shallow understanding.

However, the digital age is not without its merits. For some, online communities provide a safe space to question their faith without fear of judgment. Forums, discussion groups, and podcasts allow for nuanced conversations that might not be possible in more traditional settings. These spaces can be invaluable for young people navigating the uncertainties of belief, offering them tools to explore their questions more deeply.

At the same time, the digital age has blurred the line between personal belief and performative identity. In an era where everything from food choices to political opinions is curated for public consumption, spirituality is no exception. For many, the decision to identify as atheist or agnostic becomes a statement of who they are—or who they want to be perceived as—rather than a reflection of their inner journey. This shift raises important questions about the role of authenticity in modern spirituality.

The Digital Shift: From Intellectual Rebellion to Social Media Trends

The ways in which beliefs are formed in the digital age have fundamentally altered how spiritual ideologies, including atheism and agnosticism, are explored. Social media platforms such as Twitter, Instagram, TikTok, and YouTube have democratised information, giving young people access to a vast range of ideologies—sometimes at the expense of depth. Atheism and agnosticism, once the domain of intellectuals and philosophers, are now commonplace in viral posts and internet memes. This broad dissemination of ideas has its pros and cons. On the one hand, it allows for greater visibility of diverse viewpoints, enabling young people to be exposed to beliefs they might never have encountered in their immediate environments. On the other hand, it often oversimplifies these belief systems, reducing them to soundbites that may not reflect their philosophical depth or historical context.

For example, influencers who openly identify as agnostic or atheist often present their beliefs in stark, polarising terms, mocking organised religion, or deconstructing long-standing theological claims. While these influencers may claim to be championing free thought or intellectual rigor, the rapid-fire nature of social media often leaves little room for deep reflection or nuanced discussions. Users might jump on the bandwagon of rejecting religion, not because they've deeply studied the philosophical underpinnings of atheism, but because it aligns with the broader cultural narrative being promoted online.

The Dangers of Shallow Rejection

This moves towards atheism and agnosticism among Gen Z often lacks the same depth that past generations may have put into their rejection of religion. Previous generations who chose atheism or agnosticism were often influenced by intellectual movements and philosophical inquiry. Thinkers like Nietzsche, Sartre, and Marx, who questioned the foundations of religious belief, presented arguments that encouraged individuals to reflect critically on the meaning of existence and their place in the world. But in today's context, the rise of these belief systems among Gen Z can sometimes feel more like a reaction against the perceived failures of organised religion rather than the result of a meaningful intellectual journey.

In the past, atheism and agnosticism were responses to very real philosophical dilemmas—like the question of free will versus determinism, the problem of evil, or the existential void left in the wake of a post-religious world. These questions were not only questions of faith but of deep, fundamental philosophical inquiry. Today, however, the rise of atheism and agnosticism sometimes appears as a superficial response to institutionalised failures or to adopt a "cool" countercultural identity.

The Influence of social media and Peer Pressure

One of the key drivers of this trend is the influence of social media. Young people are exposed to a constant stream of ideas, often unfiltered, from influencers and celebrities who openly identify as agnostic or atheist. Social media has become a platform for social identity and belonging, where adopting certain belief systems can become part of an overall "cool" factor, rather than the result of critical reflection. This can encourage conformity, where the stance against religion becomes a shared norm, not because individuals have pondered the existential questions themselves, but because it aligns with the cultural narrative being broadcast.

The power of peer pressure on social platforms cannot be underestimated. In a digital landscape where likes, shares, and comments are currency, aligning with popular opinions often feels rewarding. For young people, this means that identifying as atheist or agnostic can bring social validation. However, this validation is fleeting and often devoid of the deeper satisfaction that comes from genuine self-discovery. As a result, some individuals may find themselves questioning their beliefs later in life, realising that their earlier stances were shaped more by external influences than internal conviction.

"Crisis faith" refers to the tendency for individuals to turn to spirituality during moments of hardship. While this phenomenon is not new, it has become more pronounced in the digital age, where global crises are constantly visible.

For example, the rise of mental health struggles among young people has coincided with an increase in practices like manifestation and gratitude journaling. These practices, often shared on platforms like TikTok, offer a sense of control and hope in uncertain times. However, the commercialization of such practices can dilute their effectiveness, turning them into fleeting trends rather than lasting sources of support.

Moreover, the desire for community plays a significant role in this trend. For many, rejecting religion isn't just about disbelief—it's about finding a sense of belonging in a world that increasingly feels disconnected. Online atheist and agnostic communities offer solidarity and support, but they can also create pressure to conform to group norms. In such environments, nuanced discussions about spirituality may be overshadowed by the need to align with the collective identity.

This dynamic is particularly pronounced among those who have had negative experiences with organised religion. For these individuals, the shift to atheism or agnosticism may feel like an act of liberation. However, without careful reflection, this liberation can lead to its own form of dogmatism. Rejecting religion as a reaction to its failures is understandable, but it's important to ensure that this rejection doesn't close the door to other forms of exploration and growth.

While the internet connects people across the globe, it has also created a paradox: the more connected we are, the more disconnected we feel. Online communities can provide support and validation, but they can also amplify feelings of inadequacy and comparison.

This paradox is evident in the way Gen Z engages with spirituality. Virtual spaces allow for the exploration of diverse beliefs, but they can also lead to shallow engagement. A meme about atheism or a viral video critiquing religion may spark interest, but they rarely provide the depth needed for meaningful understanding.

Ultimately, the influence of social media and peer pressure underscores the need for intentionality in shaping beliefs. While these forces can provide valuable opportunities for connection and learning, they can also hinder personal growth if they become the primary drivers of one's spiritual journey. Encouraging young people to engage with their beliefs critically and authentically is essential for fostering a more thoughtful, grounded approach to spirituality.

One way to navigate the fog of faith is to bridge the gap between traditional beliefs and modern values. This doesn't mean returning to old ways wholesale, but rather reimagining them in a contemporary context.

For example, some young people are reclaiming rituals from their cultural heritage, infusing them with personal meaning. Others are engaging in interfaith dialogues, finding common ground among different belief systems. These approaches honour tradition while embracing the fluidity of modern spirituality.

Spiritual Grounding and Reflection

As we look toward the next generation, it's crucial to ask: are we encouraging them to thoughtfully explore the roots of their beliefs? The growing rise of atheism and agnosticism could be a sign that young people are questioning long-established structures of authority, and in that, there is potential for growth. However, it's equally important that this questioning is paired with the development of a deep, personal understanding of spirituality and self. Moving away from religion should not mean moving away from purpose or reflection; in fact, it should encourage a deeper search for meaning in life—one that is thoughtful, honest, and grounded.

The concept of spiritual grounding goes beyond religious affiliation. It is about cultivating a sense of purpose and connection, whether through religion, philosophy, or personal exploration. Many young people who turn to atheism or agnosticism do so because they feel alienated from traditional religious practices that fail to address their lived experiences. While this alienation is valid, it's important to recognise that spiritual grounding can take many forms. For some, it might mean finding solace in nature or art; for others, it could involve engaging in mindfulness or exploring existential philosophy.

Reflection is a key component of spiritual grounding. In a world where distractions are abundant, taking the time to sit with one's thoughts and questions is a radical act. This kind of reflection requires not only curiosity but also courage—the courage to confront uncertainty and wrestle with difficult questions about existence and purpose. For Gen Z, whose lives are often mediated by screens, fostering spaces for such reflection is more important than ever. These spaces could be physical, like meditation centres or community discussions, or digital, like online forums dedicated to thoughtful dialogue.

Moreover, spiritual grounding does not have to be static. One of the most profound aspects of human belief is its capacity for evolution. As individuals grow and change, their understanding of spirituality can deepen and transform. This dynamic process should be embraced, rather than resisted. Encouraging young people to view their beliefs as a journey rather than a destination can help them approach spirituality with an open mind and a willingness to learn.

Finally, the importance of grounding extends beyond the individual. Spirituality, in its broadest sense, is about connection—to oneself, to others, and to the larger world. Whether through acts of service, artistic expression, or philosophical inquiry, grounding oneself spiritually can foster empathy, resilience, and a sense of shared humanity. By promoting these values, we can help Gen Z navigate their spiritual journeys with authenticity and purpose.

The Role of Thoughtful Exploration

What young people need today is an invitation to engage in a thoughtful exploration of their own beliefs, rather than adopting them because they seem "trendy" or "modern." This could involve questioning not only religious ideologies but also exploring other philosophical traditions, meditation practices, or engaging in dialogues that encourage personal growth. Thoughtful exploration requires time, introspection, and the willingness to sit with difficult questions about the nature of existence, morality, and human connection.

At the heart of thoughtful exploration is the willingness to ask "why." Why do we believe what we believe? Why do certain ideas resonate with us, while others do not? For young people, these questions can serve as a starting point for a deeper investigation into their values, priorities, and worldview. This process is not about finding definitive answers but about developing a richer understanding of oneself and the world.

Thoughtful exploration also involves seeking out diverse perspectives. In an era where algorithms often reinforce existing beliefs, trying to engage with different viewpoints is more important than ever. This could mean reading books by thinkers from various religious and philosophical traditions, attending interfaith events, or having conversations with people whose beliefs differ from one's own. Such experiences can challenge assumptions and open the door to new ways of thinking.

Education plays a crucial role in fostering thoughtful exploration. Schools and universities have the potential to create environments where students can engage with complex ideas in a supportive setting. Philosophy courses, ethics workshops, and discussion groups can all encourage young people to think critically about their beliefs. However, this requires an education system that values open dialogue and intellectual curiosity over rote learning and standardised testing.

Finally, thoughtful exploration is an ongoing process. Beliefs are not static; they evolve as we encounter new experiences and ideas. Encouraging young people to approach their beliefs with humility and an openness to change can help them navigate their spiritual journeys with grace and resilience. In this way, thoughtful exploration becomes not just a phase of life but a lifelong practice.

Conclusion: Reclaiming Authenticity in Beliefs

In conclusion, the rise of atheism and agnosticism among Gen Z can be seen as part of a broader shift toward questioning traditional structures of belief. While there is value in challenging outdated or restrictive ideologies, it is crucial that young people move beyond simply adopting the latest trends. True spiritual grounding comes from introspection, self-awareness, and a thoughtful exploration of one's beliefs and values.

Authenticity in belief is about more than just rejecting what doesn't resonate; it's about building something meaningful in its place. For some, this might involve rediscovering aspects of religion that align with their values, while for others, it might mean forging a completely new path. What matters is that these beliefs are chosen intentionally, rather than adopted passively.

One way to reclaim authenticity is by embracing complexity. Spirituality, like life, is rarely black and white. It involves grappling with paradoxes and uncertainties, rather than seeking simple answers. This approach requires patience and a willingness to live with ambiguity, but it also opens the door to a deeper, more nuanced understanding of existence.

Another important aspect of authenticity is community. While spirituality is deeply personal, it is also shaped by our relationships with others. Finding or creating communities that support open dialogue and mutual respect can provide the encouragement needed to explore one's beliefs authentically. These communities don't have to be religious; they can take the form of book clubs, discussion groups, or even online forums dedicated to meaningful conversations.

Finally, reclaiming authenticity requires a commitment to personal growth. Beliefs should not be static; they should evolve as we learn and grow. By approaching spirituality as a journey rather than a destination, young people can cultivate a sense of purpose that is both grounded and dynamic. In this way, the rise of atheism and agnosticism among Gen Z becomes not just a rejection of tradition but a step toward a more thoughtful, inclusive, and authentic approach to belief.

At the heart of faith is the ability to sit with uncertainty. Whether religious or secular, every belief system grapples with questions that have no easy answers. Embracing this ambiguity can be freeing, allowing us to focus less on finding "the truth" and more on living authentically.

For Gen Z, navigating the fog of faith is not about arriving at a destination but about embarking on a journey. It's a process of questioning, learning, and evolving—one that mirrors the complexities of the modern world.

Chapter 3

Forgotten Roots

The generational gap between Gen Z and their parents is not a new phenomenon. However, the divide has deepened in ways that seem unprecedented. At its heart lies a lack of understanding and empathy on both sides—parents struggle to navigate the uncharted waters of modern parenting, while Gen Z often perceives their parents as out of touch with the realities of their world. This chapter examines how the dynamics of parent-child relationships have evolved, contrasting the discipline-driven approaches of the past with the sensitivity-focused mindset of today. It explores how a lack of practical grounding, combined with a rise in emotional sensitivity, has created tensions that threaten to erode respect and connection within families.

The generational divide between Gen Z and their parents is stark, yet it is not a new phenomenon. Throughout history, every generation has experienced tension between the values of the past and the ideals of the future. What makes the current gap more pronounced, however, is the rapid pace of technological advancement, societal changes, and the shifting priorities of modern families.

Today's parents are often caught in the middle—straddling a traditional mindset that prioritizes discipline, respect, and a clear delineation of roles, while trying to adapt to a new world where emotional intelligence, individuality, and openness are valued. But this transition isn't always smooth. The disconnect arises because the pressures on both generations have shifted, and each side struggles to understand the other's reality.

Parenting in Olden Times: Discipline and Practicality

In earlier generations, parenting was grounded in authority and practicality. Parents were seen as figures of respect and obedience, and their word was rarely questioned. In many households, discipline was non-negotiable, and children were expected to adhere to societal norms without challenging the status quo. Emotional expression was often considered a luxury, secondary to the need for survival and stability. Families functioned within a rigid framework, where roles were clearly defined, and children were taught to fulfil their responsibilities without complaint.

Communication between parents and children was typically limited and transactional. Parents focused on providing food, shelter, and education, while children were expected to respect their elders and contribute to the household as they grew older. Cultural and societal norms further reinforced this hierarchy. In many communities, extended family networks played an integral role in child-rearing, ensuring that children were exposed to a collective sense of discipline and guidance. This "village" mentality emphasised resilience, hard work, and respect for tradition.

The emergence of technology has profoundly altered how parents raise their children. In past generations, parenting was often guided by experience and community norms. Families operated within a somewhat predictable structure, and the external pressures were fewer. In contrast, today's parents are navigating a landscape where the internet, social media, and digital devices shape nearly every aspect of their children's lives.

For Gen Z, technology is not a tool but a lifestyle. They've grown up with smartphones, social media, and constant connectivity. Their sense of self is intertwined with their digital identity, and their experiences are shaped by the information and validation they receive online. This digital immersion presents new challenges for parents who, in many cases, didn't have the same access to these tools during their formative years.

Parents find themselves in the unfamiliar position of not only worrying about the content their children consume but also about the way technology influences their social and emotional development. The line between in-person interactions and digital connections has blurred, making it increasingly difficult for parents to understand the full scope of their child's reality.

Gen Z: Sensitivity Over Practicality

In stark contrast, Gen Z has grown up in an era that prioritises emotional intelligence and individual expression. Modern parents often strive to create an environment where their children feel heard and valued, which sometimes comes at the cost of enforcing boundaries. This shift, while rooted in good intentions, has led to a perception among older generations that Gen Z lacks resilience and practical problem-solving skills. The emphasis on feelings and validation, though important, can sometimes overshadow the need for accountability and perseverance.

One of the defining characteristics of Gen Z is its heightened sensitivity to mental health and social issues. Unlike previous generations, who often internalised their struggles, Gen Z is more open about their emotions and actively seeks support through therapy, peer groups, and online communities. While this awareness is a positive step forward, it has also created friction with parents who grew up in a world where emotional struggles were dealt with privately or dismissed altogether. This difference in coping mechanisms has fuelled misunderstandings, with parents often labelling their children as overly sensitive or entitled.

Gen Z is often described as the most emotionally aware and open generation, particularly when it comes to mental health. Conversations about anxiety, depression, and identity are no longer taboo; instead, they have become essential aspects of daily life. While this openness is undoubtedly positive, it can create a tension between parents who grew up in an era where emotional struggles were dealt with privately or dismissed as mere teenage angst, and children who seek validation and understanding for their feelings.

In the past, parents emphasized resilience, the ability to "tough it out" in the face of hardship. Today's parenting style often emphasizes nurturing, emotional intelligence, and mental well-being. The conflict arises because many parents see these new approaches as indulgent or even harmful, fearing that they might create a generation too sensitive to face the world's challenges.

For Gen Z, the conversation has shifted from simply surviving hardship to understanding and processing it. Young people are taught to embrace their vulnerabilities, while their parents, many of whom grew up in more stoic environments, often struggle to comprehend why their children openly express their insecurities. This cultural shift places immense pressure on parents to adapt, forcing them to re-evaluate their understanding of emotional strength.

The disconnect is further exacerbated by the digital age. Gen Z's reliance on technology and social media has transformed the way they interact with the world, including their families. Online platforms have become their primary source of validation and connection, often leaving parents feeling excluded from their children's lives. This digital divide makes it harder for parents to understand their children's experiences, creating a sense of alienation on both sides.

The Struggle for Understanding

At the core of this generational divide is a clash of perspectives. Many teenagers view their parents as relics of an outdated world, clinging to values and practices that no longer align with modern realities. They often see their parents as authoritarian figures who fail to appreciate the challenges of growing up in a hyperconnected, pressure-filled society. This perception is not entirely unfounded; parents, shaped by their own upbringing, often default to methods that prioritise discipline over dialogue, leading to a breakdown in communication.

From the parents' perspective, the frustrations are equally valid. They see their children as overly sensitive, quick to take offence, and unwilling to handle criticism. Many parents feel ill-equipped to navigate the emotional complexities of raising a child in today's world, where even minor conflicts can escalate into significant issues. They long for the days when parenting was more straightforward, guided by clear rules and expectations rather than the nuanced balancing act it has become.

This mutual misunderstanding creates a feedback loop of frustration and disappointment. Parents feel unappreciated for their efforts, while children feel unsupported in their struggles. The lack of empathy on both sides further widens the gap, leaving both parties feeling unheard and disconnected.

The Role of Technology and social media

The digital age has added another layer of complexity to parent-child relationships. Social media has fundamentally altered the way Gen Z interacts with the world, shaping their values, behaviours, and expectations. Platforms like Instagram, TikTok, and Snapchat have become central to their identity, offering a space for self-expression and connection. However, these platforms also contribute to feelings of inadequacy and anxiety, as teenagers compare themselves to the curated lives of others.

For parents, navigating this digital landscape is a daunting task. Many feel out of touch with the technologies their children use and struggle to understand the impact of these platforms on their well-being. The constant presence of social media in their children's lives creates a barrier, making it harder for parents to connect and communicate meaningfully. This disconnect often leads to frustration and a sense of helplessness.

Despite its challenges, technology also offers opportunities for reconnection. Parents who try to engage with their children's digital interests can bridge the gap and foster a deeper understanding. Shared activities, such as watching a favourite show or exploring a new app together, can create moments of connection that transcend the digital divide.

Practicality vs. Sensitivity: Striking a Balance

The evolution from practical, discipline-oriented parenting to a more sensitivity-driven approach reflects a significant shift in societal values. In earlier times, practicality was not merely a choice but a necessity. Parents, often grappling with financial instability, societal constraints, or limited resources, focused on equipping their children with skills and habits that would ensure their survival and success. The approach was utilitarian—emphasising discipline, hard work, and adherence to societal norms. In these circumstances, emotional indulgence was often viewed as a distraction, something that could weaken an individual's ability to navigate life's challenges.

Practicality was deeply embedded in the way previous generations approached life. For instance, decisions about careers or education were often made based on stability and financial security rather than personal passion. Parents encouraged children to pursue paths that guaranteed a steady income, viewing such choices as the responsible and logical thing to do. While this practicality often led to stable lives, it sometimes stifled individuality and creativity, leaving little room for self-discovery or emotional growth.

In contrast, today's world has placed a premium on sensitivity, emotional intelligence, and mental well-being. These values have emerged in response to the growing awareness of the importance of mental health and the long-term impact of unresolved emotional issues. Sensitivity has become a necessary skill in navigating a complex, interconnected world. Individuals are encouraged to express their feelings, advocate for themselves, and seek help when needed. This shift has undoubtedly brought about positive changes, enabling people to address their emotional struggles and build deeper, more meaningful relationships.

However, the rise in sensitivity has also introduced challenges. Overemphasis on emotional well-being can sometimes lead to an avoidance of discomfort or hardship. Many young people today struggle with failure, criticism, or conflict, as they have been raised in environments where their feelings were often prioritised over resilience-building. This can result in a lack of preparedness for the inevitable challenges of adult life, such as professional setbacks, financial difficulties, or personal conflicts.

Parents today find themselves caught between these two paradigms. On one hand, they want to raise children who are emotionally healthy and self-aware. On the other, they recognise the need for their children to develop practical skills and resilience. Striking this balance is no easy task. For example, a parent might struggle with whether to intervene in a child's problem to ease their emotional burden or to let them face the consequences to build resilience. These dilemmas highlight the tension between fostering sensitivity and instilling practicality.

The Value of Practicality in Modern Times

Practicality remains an essential life skill in the modern world, even as the emphasis on emotional intelligence grows. It provides the tools necessary for problem-solving, decision-making, and navigating the unpredictable challenges of daily life. While emotional awareness is important, it cannot replace the ability to approach situations with logic, resourcefulness, and resilience. Practicality equips individuals with the confidence to act and adapt to changing circumstances without being paralysed by doubt or fear.

One of the greatest strengths of practicality is its ability to ground people. In a world increasingly dominated by abstract concepts, virtual experiences, and shifting norms, the ability to remain anchored in actionable solutions is invaluable. Practical thinkers are better equipped to assess risks, weigh pros and cons, and make informed decisions, whether in personal relationships, academic pursuits, or professional environments. This skill set can be the difference between thriving and merely surviving in a complex, fast-paced society.

Moreover, practicality fosters independence and self-reliance. Children who are encouraged to think critically and solve problems on their own are more likely to develop a sense of agency and confidence. They learn to trust their judgment, take responsibility for their actions, and persevere in the face of challenges. These qualities not only benefit the individual but also contribute to a stronger, more resilient society.

Practical individuals are often the ones who drive innovation, lead teams, and inspire change, using their skills to turn ideas into reality.

However, practicality without empathy or emotional understanding can sometimes come across as cold or unfeeling. It is important to balance logic with compassion, especially in interpersonal relationships. Parents who prioritise practicality must ensure they do not dismiss their children's emotions in the process. Recognising that emotions are a natural and valuable part of the human experience can help practical thinkers connect with others on a deeper level, fostering trust and mutual respect.

To nurture practicality in children, parents can create opportunities for problem-solving and critical thinking. Simple activities, such as cooking a meal, budgeting an allowance, or managing a small project, can teach children how to plan, execute, and adapt. These experiences instil a sense of accomplishment and demonstrate the rewards of taking initiative. At the same time, parents can emphasise the importance of learning from mistakes, showing children that failure is not the end but a stepping stone to growth and improvement.

The Role of Sensitivity in Building Emotional Connections

Sensitivity, on the other hand, plays a crucial role in fostering meaningful relationships and promoting mental well-being. It enables individuals to empathise with others, recognise their own emotions, and navigate the complexities of human interaction. In an era where mental health issues are on the rise, sensitivity is no longer a luxury but a necessity for creating supportive, inclusive communities.

One of the greatest advantages of sensitivity is its ability to build strong emotional connections. People who are attuned to the feelings of others are better equipped to communicate effectively, resolve conflicts, and create a sense of belonging. This quality is particularly important in families, where open communication and emotional support form the foundation of healthy relationships. Parents who are sensitive to their children's needs can create an environment where their children feel valued, understood, and loved.

Sensitivity also encourages self-awareness, which is essential for personal growth. By acknowledging and processing their emotions, individuals can gain insight into their motivations, strengths, and areas for improvement. This self-awareness enables them to make choices that align with their values and aspirations, leading to greater fulfilment and happiness. It also helps them cope with stress and adversity, as they can identify and address the underlying causes of their struggles.

However, excessive sensitivity can sometimes become a hindrance. When individuals are overly focused on their emotions, they may struggle to make decisions or take risks. Fear of failure, rejection, or criticism can lead to avoidance behaviours that limit their potential. Additionally, heightened sensitivity can make people more vulnerable to external pressures, such as societal expectations or peer influence. It is important to strike a balance between valuing emotions and maintaining a sense of perspective.

Parents can nurture sensitivity in their children by modelling empathy and active listening. Simple actions, such as acknowledging their child's feelings, validating their experiences, and expressing genuine care, can teach children the importance of emotional awareness. At the same time, parents should encourage their children to find constructive ways to manage their emotions, such as journaling, talking to a trusted friend, or engaging in creative activities. These practices help children develop emotional resilience and a healthier relationship with their feelings.

Integrating Practicality and Sensitivity

The key to successful parenting lies in integrating practicality and sensitivity. These qualities are not mutually exclusive but complementary, each enhancing the other when applied effectively. Practicality provides the structure and stability needed to navigate life, while sensitivity adds depth and meaning to human interactions. Together, they create a holistic approach to personal development and relationships.

One way to achieve this integration is through intentional parenting strategies. Parents can establish clear boundaries and expectations while remaining flexible and responsive to their children's needs. For example, a parent might set rules about screen time but also take the time to explain the reasons behind these rules and listen to their child's perspective. This approach shows that discipline and empathy can coexist, fostering mutual respect and understanding.

Another strategy is to encourage both independence and collaboration. Parents can give their children opportunities to make decisions and solve problems on their own, while also emphasising the importance of seeking help and working together. This balance helps children develop a sense of agency while recognising the value of teamwork and support.

Education systems can also play a role in promoting this balance. Schools that combine academic rigor with emotional learning prepare students for both the challenges of the real world and the complexities of human interaction. Programs that teach practical skills, such as financial literacy or time management, alongside emotional skills, such as conflict resolution or mindfulness, create well-rounded individuals who can thrive in any environment.

Ultimately, integrating practicality and sensitivity requires a mindset shift. Parents and children must move away from viewing these qualities as opposing forces and embrace them as complementary strengths. By valuing both logic and emotion, they can create a more balanced, harmonious approach to life. This integration not only strengthens parent-child relationships but also equips individuals with the tools they need to succeed in an ever-changing world.

The Rise of Individuality vs. Community

One of the most significant cultural shifts in recent years has been the move away from community-focused values toward a greater emphasis on individuality. In earlier generations, the family, extended family, and community often provided a support system that kept everyone grounded. Today, however, Gen Z tends to view their sense of belonging more through personal identity than through collective frameworks.

While this focus on individuality can be empowering, it also means that young people are less likely to turn to their families for guidance or support. Parents, who traditionally played the role of decision-makers and moral compasses, are now seen by many Gen Z individuals as out of touch with the realities of their world. This shift has caused an erosion of trust, with children perceiving their parents' advice as outdated and irrelevant.

At the same time, the rise of social media and online communities has created new sources of validation. Gen Z finds connection in virtual spaces, where they can find people who share their specific interests, ideas, and experiences.

Parents, who were once the primary source of wisdom and guidance, are now competing with influencers, peers, and online communities that offer more immediate feedback and support.

Reclaiming Family Dynamics

The challenge for modern parents is not simply to understand their children's emotional and social lives but to regain a sense of authority and connection. The key to bridging this gap lies in rethinking what authority means in the context of modern family dynamics.

Rather than adopting the old models of discipline and authority, parents can embrace a more collaborative approach. This doesn't mean abandoning structure or boundaries but rather fostering an environment of mutual respect and open communication. Parents can actively engage in their children's world by learning about the technology they use, the influencers they follow, and the challenges they face online.

At the same time, it's crucial for Gen Z to appreciate the wisdom that comes with experience. They may not fully understand the complexities their parents faced growing up, but by acknowledging the struggles and triumphs of previous generations, they can create space for meaningful conversations.

The Role of Mentorship

In times of uncertainty, mentorship plays a critical role in guiding young people through the challenges of growing up. While Gen Z may not always seek advice from their parents, they are increasingly turning to other figures—teachers, counsellors, or influencers who resonate with their values.

This shift presents a challenge for traditional parenting, where the parental role is central. However, it also presents an opportunity for parents to take on a more nuanced mentorship role, guiding their children through life's challenges while allowing them to make their own decisions. This form of mentorship emphasizes understanding, empathy, and trust, rather than rigid control.

Reconnecting Across Generations

The path to bridging the generational gap begins with empathy. Both parents and children need to try to understand each other's perspectives and experiences. For parents, this means letting go of preconceived notions and embracing the realities of modern parenting. It involves actively listening to their children, acknowledging their feelings, and creating a safe space for open dialogue.

For Gen Z, it means recognising the challenges their parents face and appreciating the sacrifices they make. Understanding that parenting is an ongoing learning process can help foster a sense of gratitude and respect. Shared experiences, such as family traditions or collaborative projects, can also strengthen bonds and create a sense of mutual appreciation.

The future of parenting lies in blending the wisdom of the past with the awareness of the present. By embracing both practical resilience and emotional intelligence, families can navigate the complexities of modern life while staying rooted in the values that unite them. Reconnection is not just a possibility—it is a necessity for preserving the integrity of family relationships in an ever-changing world.

Chapter 4

The Clothes We Wear, The Values We Bare

Fashion has always been more than fabric and stitches—it reflects society, values, and self-expression. In this chapter, we delve into the cultural implications of clothing choices and critique how the over-extension of Westernisation has transformed fashion into a tool for validation rather than a means of individuality. This chapter will advocate for modesty as an empowering choice rooted in self-respect and individuality, challenging the misconception that it equates to repression. Furthermore, it will explore how teenagers can learn proper ethics in dressing, emphasising the need for balanced, thoughtful decisions in how they present themselves to the world.

Fashion has always been more than just a matter of personal style; it's a living document of societal change. From the corsets of Victorian England to the power suits of the 1980s, clothing choices reflect cultural values, social hierarchies, and historical events.

For instance, the flapper dresses of the 1920s symbolized a break from traditional gender norms, reflecting women's newfound independence after World War I. Similarly, the rise of streetwear in the 21st century represents a shift toward casual, urban aesthetics influenced by hip-hop culture and youth rebellion. Understanding the historical context of fashion reveals not only how we dress but why we dress the way we do.

Today, fashion continues to serve as a form of silent communication. The rise of athleisure reflects our collective prioritization of comfort and wellness. Luxury streetwear, like Balenciaga sneakers or Off-White collaborations, communicates a blend of high fashion and subculture. But these choices aren't just about aesthetics—they're also about signalling identity, values, and belonging.

What's troubling, however, is how much of modern fashion revolves around validation. Instead of expressing individuality, many young people wear clothes to conform to expectations dictated by social media. The obsession with "fit checks" and designer labels has created a culture where status often trumps self-expression.

The Evolution of Fashion and Its Cultural Impact

Fashion, as a cultural artefact, has evolved significantly over time. In the past, clothing primarily served practical purposes: protection, modesty, and adaptation to climate. However, as societies developed, clothing began to reflect cultural identities, social hierarchies, and personal status. Traditional attire, for instance, symbolised community values, religious beliefs, and the wearer's role in society. In countries like India, Japan, or the Middle East, clothing carried profound symbolic meaning, often signifying one's connection to heritage.

With the advent of globalisation, fashion became a melting pot of influences. Western trends, propelled by media and consumerism, began to dominate global markets, diluting traditional aesthetics and values. The global appeal of brands like Gucci or Zara often overshadowed the intricacies of handcrafted garments or culturally specific styles. While this democratisation of fashion allowed for cross-cultural exchange, it also led to a homogenisation of identity, where Western aesthetics became the gold standard.

For teenagers, the rise of social media exacerbated this trend. Platforms like Instagram and TikTok created an environment where validation through likes and comments became intertwined with clothing choices. Fast fashion brands capitalised on this by providing affordable, trendy clothing designed to emulate high fashion looks. However, this shift came at a cost: it encouraged disposable fashion, reduced appreciation for craftsmanship, and fuelled an insatiable desire to keep up with fleeting trends.

The cultural shift in fashion has also sparked a conflict between individual expression and societal pressures. While teenagers are encouraged to use clothing to express themselves, they often fall prey to the homogenising forces of Westernised trends. The pressure to conform to these standards often overrides their ability to embrace individuality or heritage. For instance, wearing traditional attire may be deemed outdated or "uncool," leading many to abandon cultural roots in favour of globalised trends.

Understanding the evolution of fashion is crucial for reclaiming its potential as a medium of authentic self-expression. Teenagers must learn that clothing can reflect their values, cultural identity, and personality. By examining how globalisation has shaped their choices, they can begin to make more intentional, ethical decisions about what they wear and why.

Clothing as a Tool for Validation

In contemporary society, clothing has become an integral tool for validation, particularly among teenagers. The rise of influencers and celebrities showcasing curated wardrobes has perpetuated the idea that one's worth is directly tied to their outward appearance. For many young people, clothing is no longer about personal comfort or cultural identity—it has become a statement of status, wealth, and desirability.

Social media platforms have amplified this phenomenon, creating a relentless cycle of comparison and competition. Teenagers often feel pressured to keep up with the latest trends to avoid being perceived as outdated or unfashionable. This quest for external validation can be detrimental, leading to insecurities and a skewed sense of self-worth. The need to impress peers or gain approval through clothing choices often outweighs the desire to dress authentically or modestly.

The issue is further compounded by the influence of fast fashion. Retailers like SHEIN or H&M produce low-cost, trend-driven clothing that caters to the demand for constant wardrobe updates. While this model allows teenagers to participate in fashion trends without breaking the bank, it also promotes a throwaway culture. Garments lose their meaning, and the emphasis shifts from quality and intention to quantity and conformity.

Parents and educators have a critical role in addressing this mindset. By teaching teenagers about the implications of their clothing choices—environmental, ethical, and personal—they can encourage a more thoughtful approach to fashion. Discussions about how marketing manipulates consumer behaviour or how fast fashion exploits labour can help young people see beyond the superficial allure of trends.

Ultimately, the over-reliance on clothing for validation erodes the true essence of fashion as an art form and a tool for individuality. Teenagers must learn to appreciate that their value is not determined by what they wear but by who they are. Building self-confidence and fostering a sense of identity can empower them to resist societal pressures and embrace clothing as a medium of self-expression rather than validation.

Modesty as Self-Respect and Individuality

The concept of modesty is often misunderstood, especially among younger generations. It is frequently associated with outdated values or oppressive practices, creating resistance to its adoption. However, modesty is not about repression—it is about self-respect, empowerment, and the assertion of individuality. Choosing to dress modestly can be a powerful statement of self-assurance, signalling that one's worth is not tied to external appearances.

Modesty does not have a one-size-fits-all definition. It varies across cultures, religions, and personal beliefs, offering a wide spectrum of interpretations. For some, modesty may involve covering certain parts of the body; for others, it could mean wearing simple, unembellished clothing. The common thread, however, is the intention behind these choices: to prioritise comfort, authenticity, and respect over societal expectations.

Modesty, often misunderstood as a restrictive choice, can be a powerful statement of self-respect and individuality. In a world that frequently equates skin exposure with liberation, choosing modest attire can signal that one's worth goes beyond appearance.

This is particularly important in cultures where modesty carries significant cultural or religious meaning. Instead of viewing it as outdated, young people can reframe modesty as a contemporary choice that aligns with their values. Fashion-forward modesty is already gaining traction, with designers creating collections that prove modesty and style can coexist.

For teenagers, adopting modesty can be a form of rebellion against the hyper-sexualization and materialism that dominate modern fashion. By choosing clothing that aligns with their values rather than trends, they assert control over their identity and resist the pressures of societal conformity. This act of self-definition can be particularly empowering, fostering a sense of individuality and purpose.

Educating teenagers about the principles of modesty involves shifting the narrative. Instead of framing it as a restriction, parents and educators can present it as an opportunity for self-expression. For instance, they can encourage young people to experiment with diverse styles, fabrics, and silhouettes that reflect their personality without compromising their values. This approach allows teenagers to see modesty as a creative and liberating choice.

Moreover, modesty can coexist with modernity and fashion-forward thinking. Designers like Vivienne Westwood and Rei Kawakubo have demonstrated that modest silhouettes can be bold, innovative, and boundary-pushing. Highlighting such examples can inspire teenagers to see modesty as a sophisticated and contemporary option, redefining its place in modern fashion discourse.

Teaching the Ethics of Dressing

Fashion ethics extend beyond personal choices—they encompass environmental sustainability, labour rights, and cultural sensitivity. Teaching teenagers the ethics of dressing is vital for fostering a sense of responsibility and awareness in their fashion decisions. By understanding the broader implications of their wardrobe, they can become more conscientious consumers and advocates for change.

One aspect of fashion ethics is sustainability. The fast fashion industry is notorious for its environmental impact, from excessive water consumption to textile waste. Teaching teenagers about these issues can encourage them to adopt sustainable practices, such as thrifting, up-cycling, or investing in high-quality, long-lasting pieces. These habits not only reduce waste but also promote a more thoughtful approach to consumption.

Another critical component is labour ethics. Many fast fashion brands rely on exploitative labour practices, including low wages and unsafe working conditions. By learning about the human cost of cheap clothing, teenagers can make informed decisions about where they shop and what they buy. Supporting ethical brands or choosing second-hand options can be powerful ways to advocate for fair treatment in the fashion industry.

Cultural sensitivity is another essential aspect of fashion ethics. With the rise of cultural appropriation, it is crucial to teach teenagers about the importance of respecting and understanding the origins of certain styles or garments. Wearing traditional attire from another culture without understanding its significance can perpetuate stereotypes or disrespect the community it belongs to. Encouraging teenagers to research and appreciate diverse fashion traditions fosters a deeper respect for cultural heritage.

One of the most contentious issues in modern fashion is cultural appropriation—the use of elements from one culture by members of another, often without understanding or respect for their significance. This can manifest in runway shows, Halloween costumes, or everyday streetwear, where sacred or traditional garments are stripped of their meaning and turned into trends.

To address this, we need to promote cultural appreciation instead of appropriation. This means understanding the history and significance of cultural attire before adopting it. Fashion should be a tool for cross-cultural understanding, not a vehicle for exploitation.

Finally, ethics in fashion also involve self-awareness and accountability. Teenagers must learn to evaluate their motivations for dressing a certain way. Are they making choices to impress others, conform to trends, or express their true selves? By reflecting on these questions, they can align their clothing decisions with their values and aspirations, creating a wardrobe that feels authentic and meaningful.

Fashion and Cultural Appropriation

Cultural appropriation in fashion refers to the adoption or use of elements of one culture by members of another, typically without understanding or respect for their significance. This issue has gained significant attention, especially with the rise of global fashion and the proliferation of trends inspired by diverse cultures. Teenagers, often influenced by social media, may be unaware of the delicate balance between appreciation and appropriation when it comes to adopting clothing styles from other cultures.

For example, wearing traditional Native American headdresses as fashion accessories or donning African prints without understanding their cultural or historical context has sparked backlash. The commodification of these cultural symbols often reduces them to mere fashion statements, stripping them of their deep-rooted meaning. Fashion can become a powerful tool for cross-cultural understanding, but only if it is approached with sensitivity, research, and respect.

Teaching teenagers about cultural appropriation involves helping them recognise the difference between borrowing for admiration and exploiting a culture for trendiness. It also means promoting the importance of cultural awareness, which involves understanding the history, struggles, and significance behind certain clothing and fashion choices. By cultivating this awareness, teenagers can learn to appreciate diverse cultures without misappropriating them, celebrating their uniqueness in a way that is ethical and respectful.

Additionally, fashion brands and designers must become more transparent in their sourcing of cultural elements. Many designers have faced criticism for borrowing from indigenous or marginalised cultures without crediting them or compensating the communities for their intellectual property. By addressing this issue, fashion can move toward a more inclusive and ethically aware future, where cultural influences are shared responsibly, and cultural appropriation is avoided.

Ultimately, cultural appropriation is not just a fashion issue; it is a matter of ethical consideration. Teenagers, as the next generation of consumers and creators, must be equipped with the knowledge to make informed choices that honour and respect the cultural significance of the clothing they wear.

The Role of social media and Influencers in Fashion Choices

Social media has revolutionised the fashion industry, empowering influencers, celebrities, and even everyday individuals to become fashion icons. Platforms like Instagram and TikTok have turned fashion into a visual currency, where likes, followers, and comments validate one's style choices. However, this has created a paradox for teenagers. On one hand, social media allows them to express themselves and explore different styles. On the other hand, it places immense pressure on them to conform to an idealised image of beauty and fashion.

The role of influencers in shaping trends cannot be overstated. Many influencers receive compensation for promoting certain brands or trends, creating a cycle where clothing becomes associated with desirability and success.

Teenagers, who are still developing their sense of identity, may find it challenging to distinguish between authentic self-expression and the commodified ideal of fashion being sold to them.

As social media continues to dominate, it is crucial for teenagers to understand the influence these platforms have on their fashion choices. Developing media literacy and critical thinking skills is essential so that they can navigate the world of digital influencers and understand the ways in which social media algorithms curate content to manipulate consumer behaviour.

Influencers have a responsibility to set positive examples, advocating for more diverse body types, sizes, and cultures in fashion. As they build their platforms, influencers should prioritise authenticity over perfection and promote a healthier, more inclusive approach to style. This shift in how fashion is marketed and consumed can have a lasting impact on how teenagers perceive themselves and others.

Social media, when used responsibly, can also serve as a platform for fostering individuality, collaboration, and positive change in the fashion industry. Teenagers can learn to use these platforms to showcase their unique styles, challenge harmful trends, and embrace a more diverse and inclusive view of beauty and fashion.

The Economic and Environmental Impact of Fast Fashion

Fast fashion has drastically altered the global fashion landscape, producing inexpensive, mass-produced clothing at a rapid pace. While it has democratised access to trendy clothes, it has also led to significant environmental and economic issues. Fast fashion relies on cheap labour in developing countries, where workers are often underpaid and subjected to poor working conditions. This exploitative system raises questions about the ethical responsibility of both consumers and producers.

The rise of fast fashion has fundamentally changed the way we consume clothing. Brands like Zara and SHEIN churn out collections at breakneck speed, encouraging disposable consumption. This model not only exploits garment workers but also harms the environment, contributing to water pollution, waste, and carbon emissions.

Teenagers, often drawn to fast fashion for its affordability and trendiness, are major participants in this cycle. However, many are also at the forefront of movements advocating for slow fashion. Thrifting, upcycling, and supporting ethical brands have become ways to rebel against the system, proving that young people have the power to demand change in the industry.

The environmental impact of fast fashion is equally concerning. The industry is one of the largest contributors to pollution, with millions of tons of textile waste generated each year. The use of synthetic fibres, harmful dyes, and overproduction of cheap garments contributes to significant carbon emissions, water wastage, and landfill overflow. For teenagers, this represents a critical opportunity to rethink the way they approach fashion.

Teaching teenagers about the consequences of their clothing choices can have a profound impact on the fashion industry. By encouraging sustainable practices such as buying second-hand, upcycling old clothes, or supporting eco-friendly brands, teenagers can become part of the solution to the environmental crisis. They can also learn about the importance of buying less but investing in quality garments that last longer and have a smaller environmental footprint.

Moreover, the economic impact of fast fashion is not just about labour exploitation; it's also about consumer behaviour. The "disposable" nature of fast fashion encourages a cycle of overconsumption. Teenagers often buy clothes that they wear only once or twice, contributing to the growing issue of textile waste. The rise of "buy now, wear now" fashion culture encourages impulse buying, leading to long-term environmental harm.

In contrast, the future of fashion lies in slow fashion, a movement that values sustainability, quality, and timelessness. Teaching teenagers to embrace these principles will not only help reduce their environmental impact but also foster a deeper appreciation for clothing as something that should be cherished and preserved.

Redefining Beauty Standards in Fashion

Fashion, historically, has been tied to narrowly defined beauty standards that privilege certain body types, skin tones, and facial features. For decades, the fashion industry has reinforced these ideals through advertising, runway shows, and media. However, there is a growing movement to redefine beauty standards and create space for more diverse and inclusive representations in fashion.

Teenagers, especially, are at a stage in life where they are still forming their self-image. Constant exposure to unattainable beauty standards in the media can lead to body dissatisfaction, low self-esteem, and unhealthy comparisons. The influence of social media only exacerbates this issue, with edited and filtered images portraying an unrealistic view of beauty.

To combat this, the fashion industry must prioritise diversity and inclusivity in its campaigns, runway shows, and product offerings. Teenagers should be encouraged to embrace their unique features, from body shape to skin colour, and challenge societal norms about what constitutes beauty. In this new era, beauty should be seen as fluid, diverse, and ever-changing. Fashion can help facilitate this transformation by promoting a broader range of models, designers, and styles that reflect real, diverse individuals.

Moreover, parents, educators, and influencers can play a pivotal role in reshaping beauty standards for the younger generation. By teaching teenagers to appreciate their natural beauty and reject harmful media portrayals, they can foster a sense of confidence and authenticity that extends beyond physical appearance. Fashion should empower individuals to express themselves fully, free from the constraints of traditional beauty norms.

Ultimately, the future of fashion lies in its ability to break down barriers and redefine what beauty truly means. Teenagers have the power to lead this shift, embracing a more inclusive, authentic, and empowering definition of beauty.

What we wear affects not only how others see us but also how we see ourselves. Known as "enclothed cognition," this phenomenon explains why wearing certain garments can impact confidence, focus, and mood. For example, dressing in formal attire can enhance feelings of competence, while wearing bright colours can boost mood.

Understanding the psychology of dressing can help young people make intentional choices about their wardrobes. Instead of following trends, they can focus on how their clothing makes them feel and what message it communicates.

The Future of Fashion: A Vision for Change

The future of fashion is inextricably linked to the evolution of societal values. As teenagers become increasingly aware of the ethical, environmental, and cultural implications of their clothing choices, they will demand a more transparent and responsible fashion industry. Fashion brands, designers, and retailers will be compelled to align with these values to stay relevant in a rapidly changing market.

In this future, sustainability will no longer be a niche concern but a core principle of the fashion industry. Teenagers will lead the charge in advocating for ethical practices, from fair wages to eco-friendly materials. They will also embrace slow fashion, opting for quality over quantity and creating lasting wardrobes that prioritise longevity and timeless style.

Moreover, technology will play a significant role in shaping the future of fashion. Innovations such as 3D printing, sustainable textiles, and virtual fashion will offer new ways to create, buy, and wear clothes. Teenagers, as digital natives, will be at the forefront of these technological advancements, using them to reduce waste, personalise their styles, and experiment with fashion in ways never before possible.

The future of fashion will also be a more inclusive one. As conversations around body positivity, gender identity, and cultural representation continue to evolve, fashion will reflect these shifts by offering a wider range of sizes, styles, and cultural perspectives. Teenagers will be able to see themselves represented in fashion in ways that empower and uplift them, rather than conforming to outdated norms.

In this future-forward vision, fashion will no longer be about external validation or conformity. Instead, it will be about self-expression, individuality, and ethical responsibility. Teenagers will be the driving force behind this transformation, using their voices and choices to shape a fashion industry that reflects the values of respect, inclusivity, and sustainability.

Redefining Fashion for the Future

The current fashion landscape presents both challenges and opportunities for teenagers. While societal pressures and consumerism threaten to erode individuality and ethics, there is also a growing movement toward authenticity, sustainability, and inclusivity. By redefining their relationship with clothing, young people have the power to reshape the future of fashion into a force for good.

Redefining fashion begins with embracing individuality. Teenagers should be encouraged to explore their unique style without fear of judgment or rejection. This requires creating safe spaces—both online and offline—where they can experiment, make mistakes, and grow. Schools, for instance, can promote dress codes that allow for self-expression while maintaining a respectful and inclusive environment.

Community initiatives can also play a role in fostering a deeper connection to fashion. Workshops on sustainable practices, cultural appreciation, or DIY garment creation can inspire teenagers to view clothing as a form of art and activism. By engaging with the process of making and designing clothing, they develop a greater appreciation for its value and meaning.

Moreover, the fashion industry must step up to provide ethical and inclusive options for young consumers. Brands that prioritise sustainability, diversity, and transparency set an example for teenagers, showing that it is possible to balance profitability with responsibility. Highlighting such brands can encourage young people to support businesses that align with their values.

Finally, redefining fashion involves challenging harmful norms and stereotypes. This includes dismantling the idea that certain body types, skin tones, or genders are more "fashionable" than others. Teenagers must learn that style is not about fitting into a mould but about celebrating diversity and self-expression. By embracing this mindset, they can help create a fashion culture that is inclusive, empowering, and representative of all voices.

Chapter 5

The Woke Mirage

Introduction: The Illusion of Wokeness

In the age of social media, the term "woke" has morphed from a powerful call for social justice into a hollow badge of virtue signalling. As someone who's grown up alongside this cultural shift, I've witnessed first-hand how "wokeness" can often be more performative than transformative. The idea behind it was pure: awareness of social injustices, a commitment to challenging systems of oppression, and an unflinching desire to see change in a world steeped in inequality. But what we've seen today is a movement often more focused on appearances than on substance. The need to display one's "wokeness" online has, in many cases, overshadowed genuine activism.

While "wokeness" was intended to promote inclusivity, empathy, and societal awareness, it now seems like a contest to see who can be the most offended or who can say the right things in public. This has led to a situation where issues like race, gender, and class are discussed not with the goal of understanding, but to one-up each other in the arena of social justice. It's less about making real change and more about curating an image that fits the expectations of a society obsessed with optics.

Woke culture has become something of a catch-all label for those trying to portray themselves as progressive, but who often lack the depth of understanding required to enact lasting change. The danger here is not just in the performative nature of this movement, but in its tendency to shut down meaningful dialogue. People are increasingly fearful of speaking out or asking questions for fear of being labelled "problematic." But by focusing solely on surface-level gestures, we risk losing the complexity of these issues and failing to address the root causes of inequality.

The term "woke" has its roots in African American Vernacular English (AAVE), originally meaning an awareness of social and political injustices, particularly racism. Its rise to mainstream prominence was tied to movements like Black Lives Matter, where it served as a rallying cry for justice and equality.

However, as the term gained popularity, it began to lose its original depth. Co-opted by brands, influencers, and corporations, "wokeness" has shifted from being a call to action to a marketing tool, diluting its significance. What once symbolized resistance has now become a trend—easily adopted, often misunderstood, and frequently misused.

In the age of social media, activism has taken on a performative edge. People and brands alike use "wokeness" to signal their alignment with progressive values, but this often amounts to little more than virtue signalling. Posting a black square on Instagram or using a trending hashtag may raise awareness, but it rarely leads to substantive change.

This phenomenon is especially troubling when it comes to corporate wokeness. Many companies tout diversity and inclusivity in their advertising while maintaining exploitative practices behind the scenes. For example, fashion brands may celebrate International Women's Day in campaigns while underpaying women in their supply chains. This disconnect erodes trust and trivializes the causes these campaigns claim to support.

In this chapter, I want to unpack the contradictions and flaws within "woke" culture. I'll dive into how it has evolved, where it's gone wrong, and why it's so crucial for us, as a generation, to look beyond the surface. As someone who belongs to this very generation, I believe we need to challenge ourselves to not just participate in the performative aspects of activism but to dig deeper into what true allyship looks like and how we can contribute to real change.

The Misuse of Woke Culture

Woke culture, in its current form, is often misused by individuals and institutions seeking to capitalise on its popularity without engaging with its core principles. What was once a call to action to dismantle societal inequalities has turned into a tool for personal or corporate gain. We see companies using buzzwords like "diversity" and "inclusivity" to market their products, while their business practices remain unchanged, perpetuating the same systems of exploitation. Activism has become commodified, and the focus is now on ticking boxes rather than challenging the status quo.

The misuse of woke culture is not limited to corporations. Individuals too have begun to exploit it for social validation. It's easier to post a black square on Instagram or tweet a hashtag than to have difficult conversations about privilege or take concrete steps to educate oneself. This kind of surface-level activism feels good but doesn't result in meaningful change. It's easy to align oneself with causes when it's trendy, but true progress requires more than just aligning with what is popular in the moment.

Moreover, woke culture's focus on policing language can lead to a toxic environment where genuine discussion is stifled. People are often afraid to speak up because they fear the backlash of being called "problematic" or "ignorant." While it's important to hold individuals accountable for harmful behaviour or language, this culture of fear can inhibit open and honest dialogue. As a result, many people choose to stay silent, which only perpetuates the very issues that woke culture seeks to address.

Furthermore, the hyper-focus on language and symbols often detracts from the actual work of activism. It's not enough to say the right things or use the correct hashtags. True progress involves sustained effort, education, and the willingness to make sacrifices for the greater good. Unfortunately, the way woke culture is currently practiced often leads to a situation where people are more invested in being seen as good than doing good.

Finally, the superficial engagement with social issues has created a sense of fatigue among many. It's exhausting to navigate a world where every action or word seems scrutinised under the lens of "wokeness." This fatigue can lead to apathy or resentment, especially among those who feel they are being unfairly labelled or shamed for mistakes. The pressure to constantly perform can undermine the very activism that we should be nurturing, turning it from a genuine desire for change into an exhausting game of one-upmanship.

The Rise of Performative Feminism

Feminism, like woke culture, has suffered from its own brand of performative activism. While feminism has always been about advocating for women's rights and gender equality, the current iteration often feels more like a marketing tool than a movement. With influencers and celebrities touting their feminism online, it's become more about showing solidarity than understanding the true struggle of women around the world. It's easy to post about female empowerment, but it's much harder to confront the deeply ingrained patriarchal systems that continue to oppress women every day.

In recent years, the concept of "empowered" women has been commodified, with brands pushing products under the guise of supporting feminism. Yet, these same brands often exploit women through underpaid labour or perpetuate harmful beauty standards that contribute to the very insecurities feminism seeks to fight. This paradox—celebrating women while simultaneously profiting off their labour and insecurities—highlights the contradictions within modern feminist discourse.

Furthermore, many young people today associate feminism with a very narrow and Westernised view of womanhood. While it's important to uplift women in all their diversity, mainstream feminism often neglects the struggles of women from different racial, cultural, and socioeconomic backgrounds. Feminism becomes a trendy identity for some, but a practical necessity for others. This dissonance is a critical issue, as it prevents a more global, inclusive conversation from taking place.

The rise of "slacktivism" within feminism has also been detrimental to the movement. Much like in woke culture, it's become easier to say the right things than to take meaningful actions. Feminism has been reduced to Instagram captions, hashtags, and likes. Women often find themselves pressured to adhere to a very specific version of feminism that aligns with mainstream ideals, rather than having the freedom to define what it means to be a feminist on their own terms.

Lastly, there's the issue of tokenisation within feminist spaces. Women of colour, trans women, and other marginalised groups are often pushed to the front to make movements appear diverse and inclusive without addressing the systemic inequalities they face. This superficial inclusion undermines the diversity of thought and experience that feminism is supposed to champion. Real feminism involves not only elevating women but listening to their stories, valuing their contributions, and understanding their unique challenges.

The Impact on Society: Creating More Problems Than Solutions

Woke culture and performative feminism are doing more harm than good in many ways. While they are born out of a desire to create a more just and inclusive world, they often amplify division rather than fostering unity. By focusing on individual behaviours and micro-aggressions, we lose sight of the larger systemic issues that need attention. People are too focused on policing each other's actions and words, which results in a cycle of constant tension and mistrust.

Instead of fostering understanding, woke culture has led to a heightened sense of defensiveness. Many individuals now feel as though they cannot express themselves without being scrutinised. As a result, productive conversations about important issues like race, gender, and class are often side-tracked by arguments over whether someone's words were "offensive" enough to warrant condemnation. The focus on individual actions detracts from the collective work needed to dismantle oppressive systems.

Moreover, by labelling people as "problematic" or "privileged," we often alienate those who might otherwise be allies. Rather than encouraging dialogue and education, the focus on pointing fingers shuts down opportunities for learning and growth. We should be finding ways to bring people into the conversation, not push them away with accusations that prevent meaningful change.

The obsession with identity politics has also created a competitive atmosphere where individuals constantly try to prove their progressive credentials. This creates a toxic environment where activism is more about gaining social capital than creating real-world change. The constant need to align oneself with the right causes, say the right things, and display the right symbols leads to a kind of political performance that distracts from the real work of dismantling injustice.

Finally, this trend of performative activism has caused many people, especially young people, to burn out. It's exhausting to constantly keep up with the latest social justice issue, to stay on top of the latest terminology, and to avoid making any mistakes for fear of being "cancelled." Instead of fostering a generation of empowered, critical thinkers, woke culture has created a generation of anxious individuals who are more concerned with their image than with their impact.

Critical Thinking Over Performative Behaviour

As we look to the future, it's essential for us to move away from the performative aspects of activism and embrace critical thinking and action. This means questioning the systems that benefit from the status quo, holding ourselves accountable for our privileges, and understanding the nuances of the issues we care about. True activism requires deep engagement with the issues at hand, not just surface-level engagement that can be easily displayed on social media.

In this new era of activism, we must create spaces for difficult conversations, where people feel comfortable asking questions, making mistakes, and learning from them. We need to stop viewing activism as a competition and start seeing it as a collective effort to bring about meaningful change. It's about moving beyond buzzwords and hashtags and committing to real, tangible actions that challenge the systems of power that perpetuate inequality.

True allyship, I believe, is about listening— and learning from those who are directly affected by the issues at hand. It's about taking the time to understand the complexities of social justice rather than relying on surface-level gestures or rushing to take credit for advocating a cause. We need to move away from quick fixes and performative gestures that satisfy our need for validation, and instead, focus on fostering empathy and humility.

Critical thinking is essential because it allows us to recognise when activism becomes co-opted, diluted, or misused. We must ask ourselves, "Am I doing this because it's right, or because it looks good?" The moment we stop questioning ourselves is the moment we stop growing, and the moment our activism becomes just another box to check. Critical thinking forces us to be uncomfortable, to challenge our own biases, and to confront our shortcomings. It ensures that we don't become complacent in our desire to be seen as progressive, but instead, remain deeply committed to the uncomfortable work of dismantling systemic oppression.

Finally, we must remember that activism is a long-term commitment, not a trend. It requires the consistent effort to educate, unlearn, and engage in challenging conversations. It's about acknowledging that, while social media may offer instant gratification and a platform for our voices, real change happens in the everyday actions we take, the relationships we build, and the way we listen to and support those around us. If we're going to create a better future, it will be through sustained, meaningful work—not through hashtags and hot takes.

The Impact on Mental Health

Living in a hyper-woke culture comes with significant mental health challenges. The pressure to always say and do the "right" thing can lead to anxiety and burnout, particularly for young people who are still forming their identities.

Additionally, the constant exposure to social and political injustices online can result in compassion fatigue. While staying informed is important, it's equally crucial to set boundaries to avoid becoming overwhelmed. Activism should inspire action, not despair.

The Spectacle of "Woke" Consumerism: Capitalism in Disguise

One of the most ironic aspects of modern "woke" culture is its commodification. What began as an anti-capitalist, anti-oppressive movement has now been hijacked by the very systems it was meant to critique. Brands are now quick to slap "inclusive" or "feminist" labels on their products to profit from social justice trends. This "woke" capitalism often looks like it's aligned with progressive values but fails to challenge the underlying power structures that continue to exploit marginalised communities.

For instance, fast fashion brands proudly showcase their "sustainability" initiatives and collaborate with popular social justice influencers, yet their business model is built on cheap, exploitative labour in developing countries. What happens when activism is packaged and sold to us as a trendy accessory? This creates a culture where social justice becomes more about buying into a lifestyle than creating real change. It encourages consumers to feel good about themselves without questioning the system that allows these companies to profit off of their identity-driven marketing.

Moreover, the rise of "woke" consumerism has turned activism into a product we can buy, reducing complex issues like climate change or racial justice to a simple transaction. It's a dangerous game when companies can co-opt a movement for profit and make it seem like they're genuinely helping, when they often perpetuate the same injustices they're claiming to fight.

What happens when you buy into a movement without questioning the ethics behind it? How does our consumer-driven society dilute the power of activism and reduce it to a hashtag or a logo on a T-shirt? The real question is: can capitalism ever truly support the values that woke culture aims to represent?

Cancel Culture: Accountability or Mob Justice?

Cancel culture has become one of the most polarising aspects of woke culture, where the line between accountability and mob justice often gets blurred. It's easy to take to social media and "cancel" someone for a mistake, but this phenomenon raises important questions about justice, redemption, and the consequences of public shaming. Is cancel culture helping to hold powerful people accountable, or is it a symptom of a society that thrives on punitive measures rather than healing?

Cancel culture, a by-product of wokeness, aims to hold individuals accountable for harmful actions or statements. While accountability is essential, cancel culture often devolves into public shaming that leaves little room for growth or redemption.

This zero-tolerance approach discourages open dialogue and can create a chilling effect where people are afraid to speak for fear of being "cancelled." While it's important to address harmful behaviour, the emphasis should be on education and reform rather than punishment and exclusion.

When we cancel people for mistakes, we risk ignoring the complexities of human behaviour and the possibility for growth. Sure, there are instances where someone's actions are so egregious that accountability is necessary, but the public's rush to judge without context often leads to a mob mentality that punishes without the chance for reconciliation. Are we truly creating a culture of growth, or one of fear and silence?

This culture of instant judgment stifles open conversation. It makes people too afraid to engage in dialogue for fear of being "cancelled" over an opinion or mistake. As a result, we see people self-censoring, which only perpetuates ignorance rather than enlightenment. True activism requires us to have difficult conversations, challenge people to learn from their mistakes, and offer opportunities for growth—rather than shutting them down at the first sign of imperfection.

This section will explore how cancel culture intersects with the rise of woke identity, examining its impact on personal accountability versus the desire for public retribution. Can we reconcile the need for accountability with the necessity of allowing people to learn and evolve?

Woke as a "Personality"—Identity Politics as Social Currency

In the modern age, being "woke" is often treated like a brand or personality trait. It's not just about fighting for social justice, but about showing others that you're "aware" of the world's injustices. In this sense, being woke has become a social currency—a way to gain status or validation within a particular group. The desire to be seen as enlightened has led some individuals to perform their wokeness in a way that is more about the self-image than the actual cause.

The performance of wokeness can create an environment where authenticity is compromised. Instead of being motivated by genuine care for marginalised communities, people may start to act woke because it elevates their status in certain social circles. This performative aspect of woke culture runs the risk of turning activism into an aesthetic, where having the "right" opinions become more important than understanding the issues.

Social media exacerbates this trend, where platforms reward individuals for showing off their woke credentials—whether it's through likes, shares, or followers. But this performative wokeness often falls short of making a real impact. It encourages people to follow trends rather than challenge deep-rooted issues in society. It also promotes a false sense of moral superiority, as people gain validation without putting in the hard work necessary for real change.

How can we shift from wokeness as a performance to a genuine commitment to social justice? This subtopic will explore the blurred lines between the desire for social approval and the fight for equality. It'll examine how identity politics have been commodified in a way that distracts from the true mission of activism.

From Unity to Division: The Dangers of "Woke" Tribalism

In the pursuit of justice and inclusivity, woke culture has ironically fostered a deep sense of division. Instead of bringing people together to engage in productive conversations, we've seen the rise of tribalism, where groups align based on rigid ideological boundaries. Woke culture often thrives on the idea that there is one "correct" way to think about social issues, and anyone who deviates from that is branded as "problematic" or even "enemy" to the cause. This creates an environment where discourse is stifled, and complexity is lost in favour of purity.

We have reached a point where even the smallest difference in opinion can lead to social exclusion or public shaming. The very idea of engaging with people who have different perspectives becomes dangerous, as it risks alienating you from the "right" side of the ideological spectrum. This is not just unproductive—it's a step backward in the fight for justice. True inclusivity should mean embracing diversity of thought, not enforcing ideological conformity.

Additionally, this tribalism can lead to internalised guilt or paranoia within these groups. People begin to police each other's actions and beliefs, even within their own circles, out of fear of being accused of not being "woke enough." This division creates an environment of constant scrutiny and judgment, which distracts from the larger goal of societal unity and growth.

In this section, I'll delve into how woke culture has inadvertently fostered a climate of fear, where we're more concerned with purging dissent than with finding common ground. Can we truly build a more inclusive society if we're constantly dividing ourselves into factions over ideological purity?

The Exhaustion of "Woke" Culture: Why Activism Shouldn't Burn You Out

As the weight of activism and the expectation to stay perpetually engaged mounts, many are finding themselves exhausted by the demands of woke culture. The constant need to be on the right side of every issue, to correct every injustice, and to avoid making a misstep in the world of social justice can be overwhelming. The pressure to always be "woke" can actually make people burn out, leading to fatigue and, ultimately, apathy.

Activism should energise us, not drain us. But in a culture that demands constant attention to every social issue, we risk losing sight of why we started advocating for change in the first place. Woke culture can lead to "activist burnout," where individuals feel that they must always be performing their activism—whether it's posting the right thing on social media, attending every protest, or engaging in endless debates.

Instead of encouraging people to take care of themselves and focus on long-term, sustainable efforts, woke culture creates a pressure cooker environment where activism is treated as an all-consuming endeavour. This chapter will explore how we can balance the desire for change with the need for personal well-being. How can we create a culture of activism that is inclusive of self-care and mindful engagement?

1. Move from Performative to Sustained Action

To break free from the trap of performative activism, individuals and organisations must shift from quick, attention-grabbing gestures to long-term, meaningful involvement. The solution lies in being consistent and intentional about how we engage with social justice issues.

Action Steps:

- **Commit to ongoing education**: Learning is a continuous process. Don't just post a quote or share an article for a quick moment of visibility. Dive deeper into the history and context of the issues you care about. Take courses, attend workshops, and seek out conversations with people who are directly impacted by the issues.
- **Support grassroots organisations**: Rather than relying on corporations or celebrities to represent a cause, find and support local activists and organisations doing the hard work on the ground. Volunteer, donate, or offer your skills to help them further their missions.
- **Be accountable to the movement**: Don't stop at one post, one protest, or one act of solidarity. Consistently evaluate your actions and commitment to social justice, making sure they align with the values you're advocating

for. This is about real impact, not just temporary applause.

2. Confront the Commodification of Activism

To prevent "woke" culture from being co-opted by capitalism, we must actively resist the commodification of social justice. This can be done by supporting ethical businesses and understanding the power of our consumer choices.

Action Steps:

- **Research brands and businesses**: Before purchasing or endorsing a brand, research their supply chain and their actual commitment to social causes. Are they making a real difference, or simply capitalising on a trend?
- **Promote ethical consumption**: Advocate for and support businesses that prioritise fair wages, ethical sourcing, sustainability, and social equity. Choose companies that invest in people and communities rather than using their brand image to profit off social causes.
- **Hold corporations accountable**: Demand transparency and accountability from brands, and don't shy away from calling out performative activism. When a brand jumps on a cause for profit without any real action, challenge them to follow through or stop supporting them.

3. Create Room for Nuanced Conversations

Cancel culture often stifles productive dialogue and growth. A solution to this is creating a culture where we allow for mistakes, learning, and growth without immediately resorting to punitive measures.

Action Steps:

- **Encourage restorative justice**: Instead of cancelling individuals or groups for a mistake or misstep, promote restorative justice practices that focus on education, understanding, and healing. Give people the opportunity to learn from their mistakes and make amends, rather than isolating them for their wrongdoings.
- **Create safe spaces for dialogue**: Facilitate conversations where people can share differing opinions without fear of being "cancelled." Encouraging empathy and understanding can help people bridge ideological gaps and create real opportunities for growth.
- **Allow for complexity**: Recognise that individuals and movements are multifaceted. Don't expect everyone to be perfect or always say the right thing. Let's embrace complexity and acknowledge that everyone is learning and evolving.

4. Decentralise Woke Identity from social media

Social media has played a huge role in shaping and spreading woke culture, but it's also exacerbated its performative nature. To move beyond this, we need to engage in activism beyond the screen and create offline spaces where deeper, more authentic connections can be made.

Action Steps:

- **Engage in offline activism**: Move beyond social media activism by attending town halls, organising community meetings, and actively engaging in local issues. Real change often happens through face-to-face dialogue and collaboration.

- **Focus on long-term community involvement**: Rather than engaging in short-lived campaigns or viral moments, focus on building long-lasting relationships with communities. Work to understand their needs and contribute to the solutions that will have a lasting impact.
- **Limit performative digital activism**: Before posting on social media, ask yourself whether it will lead to a tangible outcome or if it's just about gaining likes. Focus more on actions in the real world that can truly make a difference.

5. Encourage a Culture of Rest and Self-Care in Activism

Activism should be a sustainable and fulfilling journey, not a source of burnout. Incorporating self-care into our efforts is not only essential for personal well-being but also for the longevity and effectiveness of activism.

Action Steps:

- **Set boundaries**: It's important to recognise that you can't solve every problem. Set personal boundaries around how much time and energy you dedicate to activism. You don't have to be involved in every protest or campaign to make a meaningful impact.
- **Prioritise mental health**: Activism can be emotionally and mentally taxing, so it's vital to take care of your mental health. Seek therapy, engage in creative hobbies, and practice mindfulness to ensure you stay grounded and well.
- **Rest and recharge**: Activists need rest to maintain their passion and effectiveness. Regularly take breaks to recharge, and don't feel guilty about needing time away

from the cause. In the long term, this will make you a more effective advocate for change.

6. Promote Cross-Generational Dialogue and Solidarity

Woke culture can sometimes create a generational divide, where younger people dismiss older generations or vice versa, assuming that one group is more "woke" than the other. To bridge these divides, we need to promote cross-generational dialogue and solidarity, learning from the past while forging new paths forward.

Action Steps:

- **Foster intergenerational conversations**: Create spaces where people of all ages can share their experiences, knowledge, and perspectives. This helps younger activists understand the historical context of current movements and allows older generations to engage with fresh ideas.
- **Recognise the value in diverse experiences**: Each generation has its own unique contributions to make. Learn from the struggles and victories of previous generations, while also appreciating the innovative approaches and perspectives of the younger ones.
- **Build coalitions across age groups**: Real change is best achieved when people from all walks of life unite for a common cause. Organise events and initiatives that bring together people from various age groups to collectively work toward social justice.

7. Reclaim the Concept of "Woke" for Meaningful Change

Finally, we must reclaim the concept of "wokeness" from the mirage it has become and reinvest it with its original intent: a commitment to understanding, challenging, and dismantling systems of oppression.

Action Steps:

- **Redefine woke activism**: Instead of focusing on the superficial aspects of being woke, redefine what it means to be truly awake to injustice. This involves prioritising deep reflection, self-education, and solidarity with marginalised groups.
- **Empower authentic voices**: Amplify the voices of those who are directly affected by oppression and give them the space to lead conversations about change. Let them guide the movement rather than letting it be dominated by those who are simply trying to look progressive.
- **Commit to tangible, structural change**: Rather than focusing on individual actions or symbolic gestures, commit to advocating for structural changes that will dismantle the systems of oppression we are fighting against. Real change happens when policies, institutions, and practices are restructured to promote justice and equality.

Conclusion: Moving Beyond the Mirage

As members of a generation so deeply entrenched in the digital world, it's easy to fall into the trap of performative activism. The pressure to align ourselves with the latest social justice causes, to share the right posts, and to be seen as "woke" can feel overwhelming. But we must recognise that this is a mirage—a fleeting image of progress that hides the deeper, more difficult work that remains.

True change requires more than just displaying our awareness of an issue. It demands that we engage with the complexity of the problems at hand, confront our own privileges, and take responsibility for creating a world that is more just. We must resist the urge to rush to judgment or label others as "problematic" without first engaging in thoughtful dialogue. It's through critical thinking, honest self-reflection, and a commitment to real-world action that we can begin to move beyond the surface-level promises of woke culture and work towards a society that values genuine justice, understanding, and inclusion.

The challenge ahead for us, as the next generation, is not just to be "woke" but to be awake—to question, to learn, to grow, and to act. It's time to break free from the mirage and create a world that is as compassionate as it is thoughtful. Only then can we achieve the real change that we've long been promised by the movement.

The road to meaningful social change requires a deeper commitment to activism that transcends trends, hashtags, and performative gestures. By embracing these solutions—such as fostering critical thinking, prioritising authentic engagement, and rejecting the commodification of social justice—we can build a more inclusive, thoughtful, and sustainable movement. True wokeness is not about following the latest trend; it's about being conscious, accountable, and committed to lasting change. Only through genuine effort can we move beyond the mirage and create a more just world.

Chapter 6

Lost in the Party Lights

The Hook-up Culture: A Disconnect from Self

As a 20-year-old, I've never stepped foot into a nightclub. It's a conscious choice, influenced by the overwhelming presence of hook-up culture that dominates many social scenes today. This culture seems to prioritise instant gratification over genuine connection, where people are more focused on quick physical encounters rather than meaningful conversations or emotional connections. The idea of an evening being about nothing, but fleeting interactions leaves me feeling uncomfortable. I see others dress to impress, creating versions of themselves that are more about external validation than internal identity. It's as if the core of who they are gets lost in the pursuit of being seen, admired, and desired. It's hard to participate in an environment where individuality is diminished in favour of conformity to a scene that prioritises appearances over authenticity.

In a world that demands constant productivity, perfection, and success, the party scene has become an alluring escape. The bright lights, loud music, and carefree atmosphere offer a temporary refuge from the pressures of daily life. For many, parties symbolize freedom—a break from responsibilities and a chance to live in the moment.

But beneath the surface lies a more complex narrative. The culture of partying often serves as a band-aid for deeper issues, masking feelings of loneliness, stress, or dissatisfaction. For Gen Z, growing up in a hyper-connected yet emotionally isolated world, the party lights can be both a source of joy and a dangerous distraction.

What makes this even more challenging is how normalised this culture has become. People now talk openly about their hook-ups, sharing stories like badges of honour. I can't help but feel disturbed by how disconnected we've become from the idea of deep, meaningful relationships. Relationships that are grounded in mutual respect, shared values, and emotional intimacy now seem like an afterthought. Everyone seems more focused on satisfying short-term desires, leading to a sense of emptiness when the party lights dim. In contrast, I crave connections that are built on shared experiences, trust, and a deeper understanding of one another.

The Pressure of Conformity

What strikes me most is the pressure to conform. The allure of being part of something bigger than oneself is tempting, but at what cost? I've watched friends change their behaviour, morphing into someone they are not just to fit in with the crowd. The relentless pursuit of fitting into this party culture leaves little room for personal expression. There's always an unspoken competition to be the loudest, the most popular, the most provocative. This need to impress, to be seen as desirable, can lead people to lose touch with their values, morals, and even their own sense of self-worth. I feel disconnected from this world because it seems like everyone is playing a part rather than living authentically. It's disheartening to watch people's lives be shaped by superficial expectations, sacrificing their individuality for fleeting moments of external validation.

The irony is that in a culture that seems obsessed with self-expression, true individuality is often silenced. The pressure to blend in with trends, whether in fashion, attitude, or behaviour, stifles creativity and personal growth. It's almost as if authenticity has become a form of rebellion. Those who choose to stand by their values or express their individuality are often labelled as outsiders, which adds to the difficulty of navigating this world. Yet, in my view, true freedom lies in being able to choose who we are without the burden of constant external judgment. This conformity not only stifles individuality but also shapes a toxic environment where self-worth is tied to approval from others.

The Price of Escapism

Intoxication is often the escape people turn to when reality becomes too heavy. The combination of alcohol, drugs, and the transient thrill of the party scene offers a temporary solution to deeper issues. Yet, this escape comes at a price. While others may mask their feelings through substances, they fail to address the root causes of their struggles. Over time, this pattern erodes mental health, productivity, and personal growth. It's evident to me that when people lose themselves in the haze of partying and intoxication, they forget how to function beyond the party lights. They become trapped in a cycle of escapism that only numbs their problems rather than confronting them. I find this unhealthy, knowing that real solutions come from introspection and growth, not external distractions.

The long-term effects of this cycle are concerning. As individuals continue to rely on intoxication to cope with stress, anxiety, or emotional pain, they become more dependent on these substances. This not only impacts their mental health but also damages their ability to build stable, productive lives. People begin to lose sight of their goals and the long-term consequences of their actions. The allure of temporary pleasure clouds their judgment, leaving them feeling stuck in a never-ending cycle. The rise of escapism through partying and substances also contributes to a culture of avoidance, where facing difficult emotions or situations is seen as a weakness.

However, true strength comes from being able to face life head-on, without the need to numb it.

The Loss of Respect: The Consequences of Overexposure

It's painful to witness how this constant availability to others—both physically and emotionally—leads to a loss of respect. People throw themselves into situations where they're expected to be constantly available, both to please others and to escape their own discomfort. The hook-up culture breeds a sense of disposability, where individuals are no longer valued for who they are but for their ability to meet short-term needs. The more accessible someone becomes, the less respect they command. And yet, many blame the world for failing to respect them, not realising that their own actions have contributed to this dynamic. In this environment, the lines between healthy self-expression and being exploited become blurred, and the consequences of overexposure are often felt in the erosion of self-esteem and self-worth.

It's important to realise that respect is not something that can be demanded; it is something that is earned. The more available we make ourselves, whether emotionally or physically, the less we can preserve our dignity. In the pursuit of seeking external validation, many people forget that true respect comes from standing firm in one's beliefs and boundaries. It's not about being unavailable, but about making sure that we value ourselves enough to protect our boundaries. If we constantly give pieces of ourselves away to others without discretion, we risk losing the very essence of who we are.

A Cycle of Blame

Another aspect that disturbs me is how often people blame the world for their lack of respect or emotional fulfilment, without taking responsibility for their own actions. The culture around partying and hook-ups can create a toxic cycle where people give more than they are willing to acknowledge and then wonder why they feel used or disrespected. It's frustrating to see individuals blame the outside world for not respecting them when they have normalised behaviours that invite disrespect. A lack of self-awareness in these moments contributes to a culture of entitlement where accountability is dismissed in favour of finger-pointing. It's crucial to understand that respect, both from others and oneself, is earned by maintaining boundaries and staying true to one's values, not by surrendering them in the name of temporary pleasure.

Part of this blame game is a result of the wider societal narrative that promotes victimhood over accountability. In a world that often tells people to do whatever makes them happy in the moment, few are taught the importance of taking responsibility for their actions. When people get caught up in the party culture, they may forget that their choices have consequences. The external pressure to conform, combined with an internal desire for acceptance, leads many to overlook the importance of personal accountability.

A Culture of Instant Gratification: The Cost of Convenience

The rise of instant gratification—whether through social media validation, hook-up culture, or convenience-driven lifestyles—has made it harder for people to delay pleasure for long-term gain. This has had a profound impact on our ability to focus on meaningful achievements and long-term goals. The ease of receiving instant approval or attention, whether through likes, comments, or fleeting physical encounters, has created a generation addicted to constant stimulation.

The downside is that this instant feedback loop can undermine personal growth, as we become more focused on immediate rewards rather than investing in the effort needed for long-term success.

As someone who values slow, deliberate progress in both my personal and professional life, I find it hard to relate to a culture that celebrates quick fixes. Achieving true success—whether in relationships, career, or personal growth—requires time, effort, and the patience to see the fruits of one's labour. In a world obsessed with immediacy, it becomes all too easy to forget that lasting rewards come from sustained effort and intentional actions, not from seeking quick pleasures.

Substance use is often glamorized within party culture, portrayed as a gateway to fun and freedom. But the reality is far more sobering. Alcohol and drugs, while offering temporary highs, often come with long-term consequences—physical, mental, and emotional.

For many, substance use at parties begins to fit in or to enhance the experience. However, it can quickly spiral into dependence, as the escape provided by intoxication becomes a crutch for coping with life's challenges. The normalization of binge drinking or recreational drug use within party culture makes it difficult to recognize when boundaries are being crossed.

The Impact of social media on Party Culture

Social media plays a crucial role in the perpetuation of party culture, influencing how we view social interactions and success. The constant sharing of glamorous party photos, videos, and posts creates a distorted view of reality, making it seem like everyone is living their best life while partying and being carefree. This digital façade encourages people to chase the same experiences, as they are made to feel like they're missing out on something if they're not participating in these events. The pressure to present an idealised version of one's life has led to a culture of comparison, where individuals measure their worth based on the online lives of others.

Social media has amplified the allure of nightlife, with platforms like Instagram and Snapchat turning parties into performances. The need to document and share every moment has shifted the focus from genuine enjoyment to curating a highlight reel.

This performative aspect creates a cycle of comparison and pressure. People feel compelled to attend events they might not enjoy, simply to avoid FOMO (fear of missing out) or to appear as though they're living their best life. The result is often a hollow experience—an evening spent chasing validation rather than genuine connection.

This superficial validation from social media exacerbates the problem. Rather than focusing on personal growth or meaningful connections, people become fixated on curating their digital presence, often at the cost of their mental health. The need to keep up with trends, popular party scenes, or even just seeking the approval of virtual strangers can be exhausting. This culture of constant comparison leads to feelings of inadequacy and a sense of never being enough, as people are constantly reminded of the 'perfect' lives of others.

Psychological Impacts of the Party Culture

The relentless pursuit of fun, validation, and escape takes a psychological toll. Late nights, substance use, and emotional detachment often lead to feelings of emptiness and burnout. The constant high of party culture is unsustainable, leaving many to grapple with the fallout once the lights dim and the music stops.

Research has shown that excessive partying can exacerbate mental health issues such as anxiety and depression. The disconnect between the persona people project at parties and their internal struggles creates a sense of dissonance, further deepening feelings of isolation.

Identity Crisis and Self-Worth

One of the most profound psychological impacts of the party culture is the erosion of individual identity. In a world where everyone is competing to look, act, and feel the same, it becomes difficult for individuals to hold onto their true sense of self. Constant exposure to a scene that promotes conformity—whether through social media or peer pressure—can lead to an identity crisis. When people place their worth in how they are perceived by others, especially in a party culture that values external beauty, popularity, and social validation, they risk losing the authenticity that defines who they truly are. This external validation becomes the measuring stick for self-worth, and without it, individuals may struggle with feelings of inadequacy or a loss of direction in life.

The constant need for external approval and validation can lead to a diminished sense of self-esteem. When one's sense of self is contingent on how others perceive them, it creates a fragile identity that can easily be shattered by a single instance of rejection, failure, or even comparison. This can result in a cycle of self-doubt and a warped sense of self, where individuals constantly seek validation to feel whole. Over time, this dependence on others for self-worth leads to a deeper internal conflict, as people begin to question who they are and why they behave the way they do.

Anxiety and Mental Health Decline

The prevalence of party culture, with its heavy focus on escapism and superficial connections, can contribute to increased anxiety and stress levels. The fast-paced, high-energy environment is not conducive to inner peace or stability, leading individuals to feel anxious about fitting in or being judged by others. Anxiety can be triggered by the need to constantly meet societal expectations—whether it's appearing carefree, beautiful, or successful—creating a pressure-cooker environment where individuals feel they are never good enough. This anxiety often manifests in social situations where people feel like they must "perform" or act out a role, rather than simply be themselves.

Additionally, the culture of partying, drinking, and hooking up often leads to a spiral of unhealthy coping mechanisms that exacerbate mental health issues. Individuals who use substances to escape their problems may experience temporary relief, but the psychological toll of relying on alcohol or drugs as a coping mechanism is severe. The crash that follows can bring about feelings of deep sadness, guilt, or depression. Over time, the brain becomes conditioned to rely on external substances for relief, further destabilising mental health. Anxiety can increase when the cycle of partying and intoxication leads to sleep deprivation, poor nutrition, and a lack of emotional regulation, all of which are critical for maintaining psychological well-being.

Depression and Emotional Numbness

Another major psychological impact of the party culture is the potential for depression, stemming from feelings of emptiness and emotional numbness. While the party atmosphere may initially seem exciting and filled with opportunities for connection, it often leaves individuals feeling unfulfilled in the long run. The emptiness comes from the realisation that the connections made in this environment are fleeting and lack depth. Over time, the accumulation of shallow interactions and one-night flings can lead to feelings of isolation. People might begin to feel disconnected from themselves and others, questioning the value of their social life.

This emptiness is compounded by a lack of emotional intimacy, as parties and hook-ups rarely provide the space for authentic emotional connection. Without the foundation of love, trust, and respect, relationships built in the party scene can be emotionally shallow, leaving individuals feeling lost and alone. This emotional void is not easily filled, leading to a sense of sadness and disillusionment. Depression may then take root, manifesting in feelings of hopelessness, apathy, and a lack of motivation. The pressure to maintain a "fun" persona to fit in with party culture can mask these deeper emotional struggles, preventing people from seeking help or addressing their emotional needs.

The Dopamine Loop: Addiction to Instant Gratification

Party culture is deeply rooted in the concept of instant gratification, where the pursuit of short-term pleasure takes precedence over long-term fulfilment. This culture, which promotes quick thrills through partying, alcohol, and hook-ups, activates the brain's dopamine system. Dopamine is a neurotransmitter associated with reward and pleasure, and it is released when we experience something enjoyable. However, when we engage in activities that provide instant rewards—like partying or substance use—the brain becomes conditioned to expect and crave these quick hits of pleasure.

The problem arises when the brain becomes addicted to this constant cycle of dopamine release. People begin to crave more frequent and intense experiences to get the same feeling of pleasure, leading to a never-ending cycle of pursuit without fulfilment. This can result in emotional burnout, a decrease in mental clarity, and an overall sense of dissatisfaction. The addiction to instant gratification also creates a dependence on external sources of pleasure, like alcohol or attention from others, which diminishes the ability to experience long-term happiness from deeper, more meaningful sources. As this cycle continues, people may struggle to find satisfaction in anything other than the next party or the next high, leading to chronic dissatisfaction and an inability to enjoy life's simpler pleasures.

Social Comparison and Self-Perception

Social media plays a pivotal role in shaping the psychological impacts of the party culture. It fosters a culture of constant comparison, where individuals measure their worth based on the curated images and experiences of others. Social platforms like Instagram or Snapchat are flooded with pictures and videos of people partying, traveling, and living seemingly perfect lives. The pressure to match these idealized portrayals can lead to feelings of inadequacy and a negative self-perception. When people compare their behind-the-scenes reality to others' highlight reels, it creates a distorted view of what "success" and happiness look like.

This constant comparison often results in lowered self-esteem and body image issues, especially for those who do not feel like they measure up to the standards set by social media influencers or partygoers. The need for approval, likes, or validation from online audiences amplifies these feelings of inadequacy. In addition, the relentless pursuit of social validation through likes and comments can lead individuals to feel more disconnected from their true selves, as they become consumed by how others perceive them. Over time, this digital facade contributes to a growing sense of isolation and frustration, as real-world connections become secondary to virtual ones.

Fear of Missing Out (FOMO) and Loneliness

Anxiety about missing out (FOMO) is another psychological effect of the party culture, especially when it is amplified by social media. As everyone else seems to be attending parties and events, those who opt out can feel like they are missing out on experiences that could be shaping their social lives or personal growth. The overwhelming presence of social media posts showcasing party scenes, celebrations, and group activities often leaves individuals feeling like they're falling behind or not living up to the "norms" of social life.

This FOMO can result in feelings of loneliness, as people internalise the belief that they are disconnected from the fun, exciting experiences others are having. The pressure to belong can prompt some individuals to join the party scene, even if it doesn't align with their true values or desires, just to avoid feeling left out. However, this sense of "missing out" is often misplaced, as it overlooks the fact that many of the experiences shown on social media are curated or idealised. This false narrative of a perfect, carefree social life can heighten feelings of loneliness and inadequacy, making people feel alienated or disconnected from reality.

Solutions to Mitigate the Psychological Impacts

Emphasizing Authentic Connections

One of the first steps to combat the psychological impacts of party culture is to focus on fostering authentic connections. Building relationships based on trust, respect, and shared values can help replace the shallow interactions of party scenes.

These connections offer a deeper sense of fulfilment and emotional support, reducing the need for external validation or the quick fixes of instant gratification. Taking the time to form meaningful bonds with others not only helps protect mental health but also reaffirms our sense of self-worth.

Redefining Self-Worth

It's essential to redefine self-worth beyond external validation, whether from social media, parties, or hook-ups. Focusing on inner values, personal growth, and accomplishments can help individuals build a more stable and resilient sense of identity. Therapy, journaling, and self-reflection can aid in this process by helping individuals reconnect with their authentic selves and cultivate self-compassion. Building a strong foundation of self-esteem based on internal validation, rather than fleeting external approval, is crucial for long-term psychological well-being.

Reducing Exposure to social media

To mitigate the negative effects of social comparison, reducing exposure to social media can be helpful. Curating one's online space, unfollowing accounts that promote unrealistic standards, and limiting screen time can help individuals stop measuring their worth against others. Encouraging self-care practices like mindfulness, meditation, and digital detoxes can help individuals reconnect with themselves and enjoy life in the present moment, rather than getting caught up in the pressures of digital perfection.

Seeking Professional Help

For those experiencing heightened anxiety, depression, or addiction related to party culture or substance use, seeking professional help can be life changing. Therapists, counsellors, or support groups can provide guidance in navigating the psychological challenges that arise from these environments. Professional support can help individuals process their emotions, address underlying issues, and develop healthier coping strategies. Mental health should always be prioritised, and there is no shame in seeking help to reclaim a more balanced and fulfilling life.

Building Healthy Coping Mechanisms

Instead of turning to alcohol, drugs, or party scenes for relief, individuals can develop healthier coping mechanisms to manage stress and emotional difficulties. Activities such as exercise, creative hobbies, spending time in nature, or practicing relaxation techniques can provide a healthier outlet for emotions and stress. These activities not only improve mental health but also contribute to long-term well-being, helping individuals find joy and satisfaction outside of the party culture.

Embracing Long-Term Goals Over Instant Gratification

Lastly, it is important to shift the focus from instant gratification to long-term fulfilment. Success, emotional growth, and deep connections take time to cultivate. By setting meaningful goals, whether in personal development, relationships, or career, individuals can move away from the empty pursuit of temporary pleasures. Focusing on long-term fulfilment will allow individuals to feel more grounded and purposeful, helping them break free from the cycle of party culture and rediscover a more balanced, authentic life.

In conclusion, while the allure of the party culture and its associated pleasures is undeniable, the psychological impacts it leaves behind are profound and long-lasting. By acknowledging these effects and implementing healthier alternatives, individuals can regain control of their mental health and lead more fulfilling lives.

Solutions and Reflection

To navigate the challenges presented by this culture, we must first redefine what it means to respect ourselves and others. It begins with reclaiming our individuality and setting boundaries that prioritise our emotional and physical well-being. Cultivating self-awareness and embracing the power of saying no can help restore a sense of personal dignity in the face of overwhelming societal pressures. It's essential to build a support network of friends and mentors who value authenticity over superficiality. By prioritising meaningful relationships that are grounded in trust, empathy, and shared values, we can foster a deeper sense of connection.

The next step is to engage in practices that promote mental health and self-reflection. Instead of turning to substances for temporary relief, we should focus on healthier outlets such as exercise, meditation, journaling, or seeking professional help when necessary. These activities not only improve our emotional well-being but also help us regain control over our mental health.

At its best, the party scene can be a space for freedom, expression, and connection. At its worst, it can be a trap that perpetuates cycles of self-destruction and dissatisfaction. For Gen Z, navigating this landscape requires self-awareness, resilience, and a willingness to challenge societal norms.

The lights may dazzle, but true fulfilment comes from within. By shifting the focus from external validation to internal alignment, we can transform the party scene into a celebration of life, not an escape from it.

Finally, we must challenge the culture of instant gratification by valuing delayed rewards. Success, fulfilment, and genuine relationships require time, effort, and resilience. By shifting our focus from immediate pleasures to long-term fulfilment, we can break free from the cycle of party culture and rediscover the true meaning of respect, self-worth, and personal growth.

Chapter 7

Ambitions in Chains

The Paradox of Ambition in the Digital Age

In today's world, ambition is both a driving force and a crippling weight. Social media, along with an influx of influencers and motivational speakers, has commodified the concept of success. Young people are constantly bombarded with messages that define success in terms of wealth, status, and material acquisition. What's often overlooked, however, is the toll this definition of success takes on mental health, relationships, and personal fulfilment.

The rise of the "hustle culture" is a double-edged sword. On the one hand, it encourages hard work, perseverance, and self-improvement. On the other, it feeds into a toxic narrative where success is equated with relentless pursuit, often at the expense of well-being. The desire to "make it" becomes all-consuming, pushing individuals to sacrifice rest, relationships, and personal interests for the sake of achieving an idealized version of success.

Social media has made it seem like success is just a viral post away. Stories of influencers who gain millions of followers overnight or entrepreneurs who build billion-dollar empires in a few years flood our timelines. These stories create an unrealistic benchmark, making it appear as if everyone can achieve the same success with the right "hustle." However, this narrative ignores the years of hard work, failures, and sacrifices that often precede such success.

What social media doesn't show is the burnout, the mental health struggles, or the loneliness that frequently accompany these seemingly effortless triumphs. The myth of the overnight success lures young people into believing that they're not doing enough if they haven't achieved massive success quickly. This creates a sense of inadequacy and pressure to constantly outperform oneself.

Influencer culture has created a generation that is not just focused on personal success, but on public validation. The measure of one's worth is often determined by the number of likes, shares, or comments they receive. Ambition is increasingly defined by how much attention you can command and how many followers you can amass.

However, this external validation can quickly become a trap. The pursuit of likes and followers may feel gratifying in the short term, but it creates an unsustainable cycle. The more followers you gain, the higher the expectations become. This cycle of validation can distract from authentic personal growth and lead to feelings of inadequacy when that validation is fleeting or withdrawn.

Many young people today are caught in this paradox: they chase fame, success, and admiration, all the while feeling hollow because their ambition is tethered to external validation rather than internal fulfilment. They've been conditioned to believe that without a large following or public recognition, they haven't "made it."

In a world where Instagram and TikTok glorify extravagant lifestyles and "lavish" experiences, the line between ambition and fantasy becomes increasingly blurred. Many young people aspire not to fulfil their own dreams or passions, but to live the dream they see portrayed by others online. This leads to a dangerous cycle of chasing after goals that may not align with their values, just because they seem to promise the perfect life.

This is where the conflict arises: many people know the "what" of their problems—the constant comparison, the dissatisfaction—but they struggle to understand the "why." They want the things they see on social media but can't articulate why they're so drawn to them. This leaves them confused and disillusioned, caught in a constant loop of desire for something that won't bring lasting happiness.

The pressure to attain an idealized version of success has caused a massive disconnect between real-life aspirations and the fantasies that drive them. Young people, raised on a diet of curated perfection, often find themselves feeling inadequate when their lived experiences don't match the idealized images of success they consume daily.

Social media not only feeds unrealistic aspirations but actively suppresses authentic ambition. Rather than cultivating deep personal interests or pursuing meaningful goals, many young people feel the pressure to fit into a mould of success defined by likes, trends, and viral moments.

Authentic ambition, which involves developing unique skills, pursuing one's passions, and contributing meaningfully to the world, is overshadowed by the obsession with immediate rewards. The process of striving for something—building expertise, learning from failures, and growing through challenges—is often neglected in favour of shortcuts that lead to quick recognition.

But real fulfilment, it turns out, isn't found in instant fame or popularity; it's found in the quiet, sometimes painful, but deeply rewarding process of becoming the person you want to be—not the one others want you to be.

1. The Struggle for Authenticity in a World of Unrealistic Aspirations

Social media platforms and influencer culture have become breeding grounds for unattainable standards. Everywhere you look, someone's life appears perfect – curated, polished, and packaged for consumption. This constant display of idealised lifestyles leaves individuals comparing their reality to a filtered, manufactured version of success. Many are caught in the trap of wanting what they see online, but they don't know why they want it. Authentic ambition, driven by personal growth and individual goals, is often overshadowed by the allure of fleeting trends. When influencers and celebrities constantly promote material success, expensive vacations, and superficial validation, it's easy to lose sight of what true achievement looks like.

Practical Solution: Instead of seeking inspiration from social media figures, people should be encouraged to cultivate their own definitions of success. This can start with journaling and reflecting on what truly brings joy and fulfilment, rather than emulating others. Setting clear, personal goals that align with one's values can help ground ambition in authenticity. It's essential to disengage from the dopamine-driven feedback loop and engage in activities that foster personal growth, like reading, learning new skills, or volunteering. Establishing boundaries with social media can provide space to reconnect with one's true desires.

2. Confusion and Depression: Knowing the 'What' but not the 'Why'. Many people today are deeply unhappy and have identified the "what" – they know they feel depressed, lost, or confused. But they often don't know the "why." The root causes of their struggles are shrouded in mystery, and the answers lie deeper than just a chemical imbalance or societal pressure. The "what" is merely the surface: the sadness, the dissatisfaction, the feeling of being stuck. But without examining the reasons behind these feelings – why they feel this way, what led them here, and how they can break free – they remain locked in a cycle of despair. Understanding the "why" requires self-exploration, which many avoid because it's uncomfortable. Instead, they cling to the immediate gratification of distraction and temporary fixes.

Practical Solution: Therapy or counselling can provide a safe space to explore one's emotions and uncover the underlying causes of depression and confusion. Practicing mindfulness or meditation can help people connect with their inner selves, allowing them to explore their thoughts without judgment. Additionally, writing about one's experiences in a journal can be a powerful tool for self-reflection. The goal is to create an environment where individuals feel safe confronting their struggles, rather than avoiding them.

3. The Victim Mindset: Comfort in Sadness A pervasive mentality that has taken hold of many in this generation is the victim mindset. It's easier to wallow in sadness and blame external forces than to take responsibility for one's happiness. People often identify with their pain, using it as a shield against responsibility. The mentality of "I'm so depressed because of this or that" can feel comforting because it absolves individuals of the effort required to change their circumstances. Sadness becomes an identity, a way to connect with others, and a form of validation in a world that seems increasingly disconnected. The problem with this is that it creates a perpetual cycle where individuals become so intertwined with their depression that they don't know how to function without it.

Practical Solution: To break free from this cycle, individuals must be empowered to reclaim their agency. Building resilience through small, positive actions – like regular exercise, balanced nutrition, and social connection – can help interrupt the pattern of self-pity. Encouraging a shift from passive victimhood to active problem-solving is key. Cognitive behavioural therapy (CBT) can be incredibly helpful for those struggling with negative thought patterns, as it teaches individuals how to challenge and reframe their destructive beliefs.

4. The Addiction to Self-Destruction: Intoxication as an Escape In today's culture, intoxication has become a form of escape. Whether through alcohol, drugs, or excessive partying, many choose to numb their pain rather than face it. There is a dangerous appeal in the momentary relief that intoxication offers, but it only exacerbates the underlying issues. People are seeking fleeting happiness, using substances to cope with their emotional turmoil, and inadvertently sabotaging their long-term health and well-being. What many fail to realise is that these quick fixes deepen their struggles. The emptiness that follows intoxication leaves them feeling even more disconnected from themselves and their lives.

Practical Solution: One way to combat this cycle is by creating healthier coping mechanisms. Encouraging individuals to engage in physical activities like hiking, yoga, or sports can provide natural endorphins, helping to elevate mood without the need for substances. Therapy or support groups for substance use can also offer structured environments to break free from reliance on intoxication. It's important to help people identify what they're running from, so they can face their issues head-on instead of drowning them out with temporary distractions.

5. The Perpetuation of the Negative Victim Mentality Many individuals have become so accustomed to framing their experiences as tragic or unfair that it becomes their default perspective on life. They wake up every day with a negative mindset, expecting the world to treat them badly, and interpret every situation through the lens of their victimhood. This mindset not only holds them back but also feeds into their depression. When you believe you are powerless, you cease to take action to change your situation. The victim mentality turns into a self-fulfilling prophecy, where people continuously see the worst in everything, including themselves.

Practical Solution: Shifting from a victim mentality to an empowered mindset requires conscious effort. One strategy is the practice of gratitude – taking time each day to acknowledge the positive aspects of life, no matter how small. Cognitive reframing is another tool, encouraging people to challenge their automatic negative thoughts and replace them with more balanced perspectives. Acknowledging setbacks as learning experiences, rather than evidence of failure, can help individuals feel more in control of their circumstances.

6. The Desire for Instant Gratification vs. the Struggle for Sustainable Happiness

Today's society is obsessed with instant gratification. People want quick fixes – fast food, fast results, instant fame, and shortcuts to happiness. The problem with this approach is that sustainable happiness requires time, effort, and patience. Building meaningful relationships, cultivating skills, and fostering mental and physical health are all long-term investments that don't yield immediate rewards. Yet, the pursuit of instant pleasure – through substances, social media validation, or casual relationships – has become so normalised that the idea of waiting for true happiness feels foreign and unattractive.

Practical Solution: Encouraging delayed gratification is crucial for cultivating lasting happiness. People can start by setting long-term goals and working towards them step by step, learning to find satisfaction in progress rather than the result. Fostering mindfulness practices can help people stay present and appreciate the journey, rather than fixating on immediate outcomes. Promoting a balanced lifestyle with time for work, rest, and recreation can reduce the temptation for impulsive behaviour and help individuals invest in their overall well-being.

7. Reclaiming Control: Moving from Chaos to Clarity The final step in overcoming the chains of ambition, victimhood, and self-destruction is reclaiming control over one's life. It's about breaking free from the external pressures and distractions that cloud judgment and cause inner turmoil. Reaching clarity involves confronting one's fears, taking ownership of actions, and understanding that happiness is an ongoing process, not a destination. It's a deliberate effort to live with purpose and intention, focusing on what truly matters.

Practical Solution: Building a clear vision of one's life is the first step. Individuals should be encouraged to set goals that are meaningful and reflect their values, not societal pressures. Regular self-reflection, through journaling or meditative practices, can help keep one aligned with their goals and prevent the chaos of external influence from derailing progress. Surrounding oneself with a supportive, like-minded community can also provide accountability and motivation. With consistent effort, individuals can regain a sense of clarity and direction, replacing confusion and chaos with a renewed sense of purpose.

8. Social Media's Role in Amplifying False Narratives Social media plays a significant role in shaping perceptions of success, happiness, and fulfilment. The platforms are flooded with curated content that often portrays a false narrative of constant enjoyment and prosperity. This constant bombardment creates unrealistic expectations and fuels dissatisfaction. Users become trapped in a cycle of comparison, believing they are falling short because their lives don't align with the stories they see online. The dopamine-driven "likes" and comments reinforce the idea that validation is external and dependent on others' approval, which in turn leads to anxiety and a constant need for affirmation. People fail to realise that these online personas are often exaggerated or completely fabricated, distorting reality and contributing to feelings of inadequacy.

Practical Solution: To break free from the harmful cycle of comparison, people need to practice digital detoxes—taking regular breaks from social media to disconnect and recalibrate. Engaging in face-to-face interactions or participating in activities that require physical presence and focus can reduce the grip of virtual comparisons. It's also important to follow content that promotes mental health, personal growth, and authenticity rather than perfection. Encouraging individuals to limit time on social media and unfollow accounts that perpetuate harmful narratives can help foster a healthier relationship with digital spaces.

9. The Problem with Pseudo-Feminism and 'Woke' Culture Pseudo-feminism and 'woke' culture often thrive on superficiality rather than authentic change. Many individuals, particularly young people, latch onto trendy causes or social justice movements without truly understanding the complexities involved. Instead of engaging in meaningful discussions or creating long-lasting social impact, they perform activism as a form of social currency, gaining likes and approval rather than actual change. The oversimplification of complex issues becomes a tool for personal gain, making these causes seem like badges of honour instead of deeply ingrained values. This shallow approach to activism distracts from real societal problems and encourages a culture of performative allyship rather than genuine progress.

Practical Solution: Education is the key to overcoming the emptiness of pseudo-feminism and 'woke' culture. People need to engage in critical thinking and dive deeper into the complexities of social justice issues rather than adopting them for the sake of appearance. This can be achieved through reading, attending talks, and engaging in authentic conversations with people from diverse backgrounds. True activism comes from understanding the root causes of inequality and working towards systemic change, not simply participating in trending hashtags.

10. The Perils of Chasing Fame Over Fulfilment The pursuit of fame, whether on social media or through traditional celebrity routes, has become a dominant goal for many in today's world. People often sacrifice their privacy, integrity, and well-being in exchange for temporary recognition. The emphasis on outward success, driven by likes, followers, and brand collaborations, distorts the importance of personal fulfilment. True happiness comes from inner peace, meaningful relationships, and a sense of purpose, not from the ephemeral nature of fame. When people place their worth on external validation, they begin to define themselves by how others perceive them, losing touch with their authentic selves in the process.

Practical Solution: To counter the desire for fame, individuals should be encouraged to focus on intrinsic goals that bring them satisfaction and joy. This includes nurturing relationships, learning new skills, and finding purpose in work or hobbies. Building self-esteem from internal sources, such as personal accomplishments and self-reflection, can help reduce the dependence on external recognition. Meditation, self-compassion, and spending time with loved ones can foster a deeper connection with one's true self and lead to fulfilment beyond the superficial pursuit of fame.

11. The Dangers of Validation-Seeking Behaviours In today's world, seeking validation has become second nature for many individuals. Social media platforms have turned validation into a commodity, where likes, shares, and comments equate to self-worth. This constant need for external approval can erode one's sense of self and create anxiety when validation is not received. When validation becomes the primary source of self-esteem, individuals begin to perform rather than live authentically, adjusting their behaviour and opinions to fit the expectations of others. This behaviour can lead to a loss of personal identity, as individuals are no longer making decisions based on what they truly want, but rather on what will garner the most approval.

Practical Solution: Learning to seek internal validation rather than external approval is a transformative step in overcoming validation-seeking behaviours. Practicing self-affirmations, developing self-confidence through small successes, and setting personal goals can build a sense of worth that is independent of others' opinions. Encouraging people to embrace their individuality and prioritise their own values over external praise can help them feel more grounded and self-assured. Therapy or support groups that focus on building self-esteem can also be a valuable resource for individuals struggling with validation-seeking tendencies.

12. The Role of Escapism in Self-Sabotage Escapism, whether through substance use, excessive partying, or digital distractions, has become a common coping mechanism for dealing with dissatisfaction and unresolved issues. While these activities may offer short-term relief, they ultimately perpetuate feelings of emptiness and self-sabotage. Escaping reality prevents individuals from confronting their problems, delaying the process of self-healing and growth. It's easier to numb emotional pain than to face it, but this behaviour only deepens the emotional void. Over time, the reliance on escapism becomes a dangerous cycle, with individuals losing touch with their goals, aspirations, and true selves.

Practical Solution: To break the cycle of escapism, individuals need to replace harmful distractions with healthy, engaging activities. Developing hobbies that foster creativity or physical well-being, like painting, running, or cooking, can provide a positive outlet for stress. Seeking professional help to address the root causes of escapism is essential, as it helps individuals explore healthier coping mechanisms. Creating a daily routine that incorporates self-care and goal setting can give individuals a sense of control, reducing the temptation to escape through substances or unhealthy behaviours.

13. The Impact of Instant Gratification on Long-Term Health The desire for instant gratification, from food to entertainment, has long-term consequences on physical and mental health. The constant pursuit of immediate pleasure leads to poor habits, such as overeating, lack of exercise, and insufficient sleep. This can manifest in mental health issues like anxiety, depression, and burnout. The inability to delay gratification prevents individuals from engaging in activities that require sustained effort and commitment, like building a career or maintaining meaningful relationships. When everything is about instant rewards, individuals struggle to appreciate the process and the growth that comes from perseverance.

Practical Solution: Building resilience against the temptation of instant gratification requires developing patience and self-control. People can start by setting small, achievable goals that require effort over time. For example, committing to regular exercise, practicing mindfulness, or pursuing long-term projects can teach individuals the value of sustained effort. Practicing gratitude for small milestones can help individuals stay motivated and appreciate the journey, rather than fixating on immediate rewards. Support systems, such as accountability partners or coaches, can also help individuals stay on track with their long-term health and personal goals.

14. The False Comfort of Sadness and the Need for Healing Many individuals find comfort in their sadness, as it becomes a familiar, safe space. It's easy to identify with sadness because it is tangible and constant. In a world where everything feels uncertain, sadness provides a false sense of stability. It's a feeling that people can hold onto, as painful as it is, because it seems more predictable than the unknown. However, remaining in sadness prevents individuals from healing and moving forward. True emotional growth comes from processing grief and pain, not from holding onto them. The idea that one must always be sad to be understood or validated can perpetuate a cycle of negativity that hinders recovery.

Practical Solution: Healing from sadness requires a willingness to embrace discomfort and seek professional help. Therapy, support groups, and engaging in self-care routines can provide tools for individuals to process their emotions in a healthy way. It's important to help people understand that healing is a journey, and it's okay to not feel happy all the time. Practices like mindfulness, breathing exercises, and journaling can help individuals feel more connected to their emotions and begin the process of moving beyond their sadness. Encouraging self-compassion is crucial in allowing people to forgive themselves for feeling down and take active steps toward emotional wellness.

Chapter 8

Situation ships and the Death of Respect

1. The Concept of situation ships

Situation ships are defined by their lack of structure. Unlike traditional relationships where roles and expectations are clear, situation ships thrive on ambiguity, often leaving individuals unsure of where they stand. This uncertainty breeds insecurity and stifles emotional growth, leading to unhealthy attachments that are neither fulfilling nor stable. The lack of defined boundaries creates a sense of confusion, which can be emotionally exhausting for those involved, preventing them from forming real, lasting connections.

Furthermore, situation ships often lead to a diminished sense of self-worth. The lack of clarity in these relationships makes it difficult for individuals to prioritise their own emotional needs. In the absence of mutual commitment and accountability, people in situation ships may find themselves emotionally invested without the reassurance of reciprocation. This emotional imbalance fosters a sense of insecurity, where one person may feel disposable or unimportant. Over time, this dynamic erodes the potential for genuine intimacy.

The unpredictability of situation ships also breeds anxiety. Without the safety net of commitment, individuals are left wondering whether their feelings will be validated or dismissed. This constant state of uncertainty can prevent people from fully investing in the relationship, out of fear that it will end abruptly without closure. As a result, individuals may become emotionally guarded, reluctant to open and show vulnerability for fear of being hurt.

In today's dating landscape, the term "situationship" has become increasingly common, particularly among younger generations. A situationship is a romantic or sexual relationship that lacks the commitment and clear boundaries of a traditional relationship. It's an ambiguous, often undefined connection that can exist for months, even years, with neither party willing to define it.

Situationships thrive in an era where instant gratification and casual encounters are normalized. The advent of dating apps, social media, and the casual hook-up culture have all contributed to the rise of these relationships, where labels and commitment are often avoided. The lack of definition gives both parties freedom, but it also creates confusion and emotional turbulence.

For many, situationships offer the allure of closeness without the weight of responsibility or expectations. It's a form of romantic engagement that allows individuals to enjoy intimacy and companionship while avoiding the potential emotional costs of a committed relationship. However, this seemingly carefree setup often comes with underlying issues that can lead to heartache, confusion, and a gradual erosion of mutual respect.

Lastly, situation ships offer a false sense of freedom. While the lack of commitment might seem liberating, it often leads to deeper emotional dissatisfaction. People in these arrangements may convince themselves they are avoiding the responsibilities of a "real" relationship, but they are denying themselves the chance to form meaningful bonds. Over time, the emotional void created by this lack of connection can lead to feelings of loneliness and regret.

2. Loss of Respect in Modern Dating

The foundation of respect has been chipped away by a culture that prioritises instant gratification over meaningful connection. In today's dating scene, many individuals treat relationships as disposable, leading to a lack of investment in the emotional needs of their partners. The rise of casual encounters, enabled by dating apps and social media, has led to an environment where respect is seen as optional rather than essential. The act of ghosting, for instance, is often considered an acceptable way to end a relationship, further degrading the importance of mutual respect.

In a broader cultural context, the rise of situation ships signals a shift in how we understand relationships and respect. In the past, relationships were often based on clear mutual understanding and respect. Commitment, while not without its challenges, was rooted in the idea that both individuals prioritized each other's emotional well-being.

Today, however, respect in relationships has been redefined. Rather than being seen as a fundamental pillar of connection, respect has been relegated to a secondary concern—often overshadowed by the desire for personal freedom, convenience, and instant gratification. This shift reflects a cultural change that prioritizes individual needs over collective respect and understanding.

The death of respect is not limited to romantic situation ships. It permeates broader social interactions, where transactional relationships and surface-level connections are prioritized over genuine emotional investment. As a result, the very concept of respect has been diluted, leaving behind a culture where emotional depth is sacrificed for convenience and short-term pleasure

This disregard for respect also manifests in the way people communicate. Instead of engaging in open, honest conversations about their feelings, many individuals prefer to avoid confrontation altogether. This avoidance behaviour can lead to a breakdown in communication, where misunderstandings go unresolved, and feelings are left unexpressed. The lack of respect for one another's emotions breeds a culture of emotional neglect, leaving individuals feeling unheard and unimportant.

In addition, the erosion of respect in modern dating leads to a superficial approach to relationships. With the rise of "swipe culture," people often view others as mere options, rather than fully formed individuals with emotions and needs. This objectification not only dehumanises individuals but also prevents genuine emotional connections from forming. Without mutual respect, relationships become transactional rather than meaningful, leaving both parties feeling unsatisfied and unfulfilled.

Lastly, the diminishing respect for one another leads to unhealthy relationship patterns. When respect is absent, individuals may engage in toxic behaviours such as manipulation, dishonesty, or controlling actions. These behaviours, when unchecked, can escalate into emotional abuse, causing long-term damage to both parties. The absence of respect in relationships creates a dangerous cycle of emotional harm that is difficult to break once it has taken root.

3. Commitment Issues: The Fear of Vulnerability

In a world that celebrates independence and individualism, commitment has become a rarity. The fear of vulnerability is one of the key reasons people avoid committing to serious relationships. When individuals are afraid to open and expose their true selves, they often choose to remain in shallow, noncommittal relationships that offer safety from emotional exposure. This fear of vulnerability can be traced back to early experiences of rejection or betrayal, which make it difficult to trust others.

Commitment issues are further exacerbated by the pressure to maintain a certain level of independence. In modern society, individuals are often encouraged to prioritise personal goals and self-fulfilment over relationships, leading to a mindset where commitment is seen as a threat to personal freedom. This belief that commitment will limit one's autonomy prevents people from fully investing in their relationships, leaving them feeling disconnected and unfulfilled.

Moreover, the constant availability of potential partners through dating apps and social media makes it easier for individuals to avoid commitment altogether. The fear of missing out (FOMO) leads many to think that they might find someone better or more compatible if they wait. This mentality prevents people from nurturing the relationships they already have, making it difficult to form lasting connections. As a result, many individuals end up feeling stuck in a cycle of short-term relationships that lack depth and emotional fulfilment.

Finally, commitment issues can have a lasting psychological impact. Individuals who avoid commitment often struggle with feelings of loneliness and isolation, despite being surrounded by potential partners. They may experience a sense of disconnection from others, which leads to emotional numbness. Over time, this can result in a fear of true intimacy, where individuals become afraid of getting close to others for fear of being hurt or abandoned.

4. Cheating and the Diminishment of Trust

Cheating has become normalised in many relationships, even outside the context of situation ships. What was once considered a betrayal of trust has become a common occurrence in modern dating. The advent of social media and dating apps has made it easier than ever for people to engage in infidelity, often without the knowledge of their partners. This behaviour undermines the very foundation of a relationship, leading to emotional distress, broken trust, and the erosion of respect.

The psychological impact of cheating is profound. For the betrayed partner, infidelity causes deep emotional pain, often resulting in feelings of inadequacy, shame, and anger. Trust, once broken, is incredibly difficult to rebuild. The process of rebuilding trust requires transparency, honesty, and accountability—qualities that are often missing in relationships characterised by cheating. This emotional turmoil can lead to long-term issues with self-esteem and a fear of future betrayal.

Furthermore, cheating reflects a lack of respect for both the partner and the relationship. It suggests that one person values their own desires over the emotional well-being of their partner. This selfishness creates a toxic environment where communication breaks down, and emotional needs go unmet. The cheater may rationalise their actions, but the reality is that cheating causes deep emotional damage, both to the victim and the perpetrator, creating a cycle of distrust and emotional instability.

In some cases, the trauma caused by cheating can lead individuals to engage in unhealthy relationship patterns in the future. Betrayed partners may develop trust issues or fear intimacy, preventing them from forming meaningful connections. On the other hand, those who cheat may struggle with guilt and a lack of self-respect, perpetuating a cycle of dishonesty and emotional harm. The consequences of cheating are far-reaching, affecting not just the individuals involved but also their future relationships and emotional health.

5. The Rise of 'Casual' Relationships and Their Consequences

Casual relationships, often dismissed as inconsequential, may seem harmless on the surface. However, they can have long-term psychological effects, creating a disconnect between physical intimacy and emotional attachment. In an era where hook-ups and casual encounters have become more socially acceptable, many individuals fail to recognise the emotional consequences of engaging in these types of relationships. The absence of emotional commitment in casual relationships leads to the potential for confusion and emotional neglect, as people may develop feelings that are not reciprocated or acknowledged.

The psychological toll of casual relationships often manifests as feelings of emptiness and loneliness. Although people may engage in physical intimacy, they may struggle to find emotional fulfilment. Over time, this lack of genuine emotional connection can erode one's self-worth, as the individual may begin to internalise the belief that they are only worthy of fleeting, non-committed interactions. This creates a sense of emotional disconnection, leaving people feeling more isolated despite their physical closeness with others.

Moreover, casual relationships often reinforce unrealistic expectations about love and intimacy. The lack of emotional depth and commitment may lead individuals to believe that genuine relationships are unnecessary or unrealistic. This attitude can prevent people from forming meaningful connections and discourage them from putting in the effort required to maintain a healthy, committed relationship. It fosters a sense of emotional detachment that can carry over into other aspects of life, ultimately hindering emotional growth.

In addition, the normalisation of casual relationships contributes to a culture where emotional vulnerability is avoided. Many people enter into casual relationships as a defence mechanism, protecting themselves from the potential pain of rejection or heartbreak. However, this avoidance of vulnerability often prevents individuals from developing the emotional resilience needed to sustain a lasting, committed relationship. Without the willingness to be vulnerable and emotionally invested, individuals may miss out on the deeper, more fulfilling connections that are possible through authentic love.

6. Ghosting: The Ultimate Form of Disrespect

Ghosting—the act of suddenly cutting off all communication with someone—has become one of the most hurtful and disrespectful behaviours in modern dating. This practice occurs when one person abruptly disappears from a relationship or potential relationship without explanation, leaving the other person confused, hurt, and abandoned. Ghosting is particularly damaging because it leaves no closure and provides no opportunity for the affected person to process the relationship or its end. Instead, the ghosted individual is left grappling with unanswered questions and feelings of rejection.

The psychological impact of ghosting is significant. For the person who is ghosted, it can lead to a loss of self-worth and increased anxiety. The lack of closure often results in a lingering sense of confusion, with the individual replaying events and wondering what went wrong. This can lead to feelings of inadequacy or self-doubt, as the person may start to question their own value or attractiveness. Over time, the trauma of being ghosted can result in difficulties trusting others and an increased fear of future rejection.

Ghosting also undermines the principles of communication and respect in relationships. The failure to communicate openly and honestly is an act of avoidance, often reflecting a lack of maturity or emotional intelligence. It sends a message that the person doing the ghosting is unwilling to take responsibility for their actions or feelings, which further diminishes the trust and respect that are necessary for a healthy relationship. The avoidance of direct confrontation, while seemingly easier in the moment, can cause long-lasting emotional harm.

Furthermore, the prevalence of ghosting in modern dating exacerbates the fear of vulnerability. When people experience the sting of being ghosted, they often become emotionally guarded in future relationships. The fear of being left without explanation or closure can prevent individuals from opening to others, hindering the development of meaningful emotional connections. As a result, the cycle of ghosting perpetuates a culture of emotional unavailability and detachment, making it harder for individuals to build trust and intimacy in their future relationships.

7. The Impact of Emotional Unavailability

Emotional unavailability is a hallmark of situation ships and casual dating. When one or both partners are emotionally distant, it prevents meaningful connections from forming. This emotional detachment is often a defence mechanism used to avoid the vulnerability and potential pain of emotional closeness. In situation ships, emotional unavailability is often a strategy to maintain independence while avoiding the complexities of true emotional commitment. Unfortunately, this lack of emotional engagement leaves individuals feeling unfulfilled and disconnected.

The psychological impact of emotional unavailability can be profound. For the person seeking emotional intimacy, the lack of reciprocity leads to feelings of rejection and isolation. This imbalance can create a deep sense of dissatisfaction, where one partner is invested in the relationship emotionally, but the other remains distant or detached. Over time, this dynamic can lead to emotional burnout, as the invested partner becomes frustrated with the lack of connection and the inability to communicate their needs.

Additionally, emotional unavailability can result in a lack of self-awareness and personal growth. Without the opportunity to engage in deep, honest conversations about feelings and needs, individuals in emotionally unavailable relationships may struggle to understand themselves and their own emotional needs. This stunted emotional growth can prevent them from forming healthier, more fulfilling relationships in the future, as they become accustomed to shallow interactions that lack depth or authenticity.

Finally, the consequences of emotional unavailability extend beyond romantic relationships. This pattern of emotional avoidance can spill over into other areas of life, affecting friendships, family dynamics, and even professional relationships. When individuals become accustomed to emotional detachment, they may struggle to connect with others on a deeper level, leading to a pervasive sense of isolation and a lack of fulfilment in various aspects of life. As emotional availability is essential for building strong, supportive relationships, its absence creates a barrier to emotional intimacy and connection.

8. The Illusion of Instant Gratification

Modern dating apps and social media have created an environment where instant gratification is the norm. This constant access to potential partners and the ease with which people can find attention and validation has made it more difficult to foster meaningful relationships. Rather than taking the time to get to know someone and invest emotionally, individuals are often looking for the next "quick fix" of validation—whether through likes, matches, or compliments. This behaviour erodes the patience and effort that used to be required to build genuine connections.

The psychological impact of this instant gratification culture is evident in how relationships are approached. People become conditioned to expect immediate results, whether it's receiving a response to a message, getting a match on a dating app, or having their needs met quickly. When relationships don't follow this rapid pace, individuals can become frustrated or disillusioned. This lack of patience can lead to a diminished capacity for long-term commitment, as people struggle to invest in relationships that require emotional work and time.

Furthermore, the constant pursuit of instant gratification diminishes the satisfaction that comes from building something meaningful over time. When everything is immediate and easily accessible, it becomes more difficult to appreciate the value of slow, steady emotional connection. This creates a culture of superficiality, where people are more interested in fleeting moments of pleasure than in building lasting emotional bonds. As a result, many individuals find themselves in relationships that lack depth and fulfilment.

Lastly, the pursuit of instant gratification can hinder emotional maturity. In relationships, emotional growth and understanding often require time and patience. However, when individuals are conditioned to expect quick results, they may avoid the discomfort of emotional challenges that are essential for deepening a connection. This avoidance of discomfort prevents individuals from developing the resilience and emotional intelligence needed to navigate the complexities of a committed relationship.

9. The Toxicity of 'Talking' Without Commitment

The culture of "talking" has replaced traditional dating in many circles, where individuals casually interact, often on a regular basis, without ever labelling the relationship. This ambiguity breeds toxicity, as one or both parties may develop feelings or expectations that are never explicitly communicated. The lack of clear commitment often leads to resentment, confusion, and unspoken emotional needs that are never addressed. While some may argue that "talking" allows for freedom, it often results in emotional stagnation, as neither person feels the responsibility to nurture or respect the connection.

Psychologically, the "talking" phase fosters insecurity. The lack of clarity prevents individuals from feeling secure in their emotional investments, making them second-guess their place in the other person's life. This uncertainty can lead to overthinking, anxiety, and emotional distress, as individuals try to decipher the other person's intentions. The confusion about where they stand can undermine their self-esteem, leaving them questioning their value or desirability. It also creates a sense of emotional neglect, as the person may feel like they're being kept on the back burner or not prioritised.

Another consequence of "talking" without commitment is the delayed emotional intimacy. Without clear intentions or mutual understanding, emotional barriers remain intact, preventing genuine connection. People in these types of situations often avoid deeper conversations about values, goals, and desires, keeping the relationship on a superficial level. This superficial connection, while seemingly satisfying in the moment, never allows for the growth of trust or emotional safety, both of which are necessary for a deeper, more fulfilling relationship. As a result, individuals in these scenarios may feel emotionally empty despite spending significant time with someone.

Lastly, this lack of commitment can negatively impact future relationships. Individuals who experience the emotional turmoil of ambiguous "talking" phases may develop trust issues or a fear of commitment in future relationships. The emotional scars left by such experiences can cause people to become emotionally distant, reluctant to fully engage with someone new. The residue of past "talking" relationships often creates hesitancy toward authenticity, making it difficult to move past the shallow patterns established in previous encounters.

10. Commitment to Convenience Over Connection

In an age where convenience is often prioritised, many individuals opt for relationships that are easy and require minimal emotional investment. This preference for convenience over genuine connection leads to a proliferation of relationships that lack depth and mutual understanding. While convenient relationships may seem appealing in the short term, they are ultimately unsustainable because they do not foster the emotional intimacy necessary for long-lasting connections. People in these relationships may avoid confrontation, avoid discussing their feelings, and generally avoid doing the work that relationships demand.

Psychologically, this avoidance of emotional depth can lead to a sense of dissatisfaction and unfulfillment. The lack of emotional engagement creates a void that superficial interactions cannot fill. Individuals in convenient relationships often experience a sense of emotional numbness, as they fail to develop the emotional bonds necessary for a true connection. Over time, this lack of fulfilment leads to feelings of loneliness and disconnection, even when physically close to another person.

The pursuit of convenience also fosters a lack of accountability. When individuals settle for relationships that are easy and require little emotional effort, they tend to ignore or downplay the importance of mutual respect, communication, and effort. This lack of accountability can result in a breakdown of trust and a general disregard for each other's emotional well-being. The failure to prioritise the emotional needs of a partner creates an environment where both parties feel undervalued and overlooked.

Furthermore, this mindset of convenience can have negative consequences on self-worth. When individuals engage in relationships that prioritise convenience over authenticity, they may start to believe that they are not worthy of the effort it takes to build a deeper connection. This can lead to feelings of inadequacy and insecurity, which affect future relationships. The psychological damage caused by settling for relationships based on convenience can cause individuals to doubt their own emotional needs, often leading them to accept less than they deserve.

11. The Influence of social media on Relationship Standards

Social media plays a pivotal role in shaping modern relationship dynamics, often promoting unrealistic ideals of love and intimacy. Platforms like Instagram, TikTok, and Facebook frequently showcase polished images of relationships, emphasising superficial perfection over the raw, unfiltered reality. These portrayals create unrealistic expectations, where individuals may believe that relationships should always be exciting, visually appealing, and without conflict. This distorted view of relationships pressures people to seek out connections that are based on external validation rather than genuine emotional compatibility.

Psychologically, the impact of social media on relationships is profound. When individuals compare their real relationships to the curated, idealised versions they see online, they often feel inadequate or dissatisfied. Social media fosters a false narrative that everyone else is in a perfect relationship, leading to feelings of loneliness, jealousy, and insecurity. These unrealistic expectations also lead to dissatisfaction in one's own relationship, as the individual may feel like their relationship is lacking in comparison.

Furthermore, the culture of comparison on social media undermines the ability to appreciate one's own relationship. Instead of celebrating the unique aspects of their bond, individuals may become preoccupied with how their relationship measures up to others. This constant comparison creates a sense of emotional disconnect, as people become more focused on external approval than internal connection. It also leads to an unrealistic sense of entitlement, where individuals expect their relationships to be flawless, forgetting that true connection is rooted in vulnerability, conflict resolution, and growth.

In addition, social media's role in amplifying shallow relationships cannot be ignored. The constant availability of attention and validation through likes, comments, and direct messages encourages people to seek affirmation from external sources, rather than nurturing the intimacy in their actual relationships. This reliance on external validation distorts the perception of what a meaningful connection should look like, replacing emotional depth with temporary satisfaction.

As a result, social media perpetuates a cycle of superficial relationships that lack the emotional commitment necessary for long-term happiness.

12. The Desensitisation to Emotional Intimacy

As modern relationships become more casual and less emotionally involved, individuals have become increasingly desensitised to emotional intimacy. Intimacy, once considered a vital component of a committed relationship, has been diluted by the rise of fleeting encounters and emotional unavailability. People are now more likely to engage in physical relationships without forming emotional bonds, leading to an overall devaluation of emotional closeness. This detachment has serious consequences for mental health and the ability to form meaningful connections.

The psychological impact of desensitisation to emotional intimacy is significant. Individuals may begin to perceive emotional closeness as unnecessary or burdensome, preferring the ease of surface-level interactions. Over time, this aversion to vulnerability can cause individuals to become emotionally distant, even in relationships where there is potential for deeper connection. The fear of opening and exposing one's true feelings creates a barrier to emotional intimacy, preventing the relationship from progressing into something more meaningful.

Moreover, desensitisation to emotional intimacy leads to emotional numbness. When individuals become accustomed to shallow relationships, they lose the ability to experience the depth of connection that comes with true intimacy. This emotional numbness can manifest as a general dissatisfaction with relationships, as people feel disconnected or unfulfilled despite their physical or social closeness with others. Over time, this numbness can turn into apathy, leaving individuals with a hollow sense of loneliness and a growing inability to connect with others on a deeper level.

This lack of emotional intimacy also has long-term implications for one's mental health. Research has shown that emotional connection is a fundamental human need, and its absence can lead to feelings of depression, anxiety, and isolation. When individuals are unable to experience emotional closeness in their relationships, they may struggle with feelings of inadequacy or unworthiness. This emotional disconnect can prevent individuals from developing healthy, supportive relationships, perpetuating a cycle of loneliness and emotional neglect.

13. Commitment Issues: Fear of Being Vulnerable

Commitment issues often stem from a deep fear of vulnerability. Today, the emphasis on independence and self-reliance has led many individuals to view commitment as a form of emotional dependence. Rather than seeing commitment as a mutual bond of trust and respect, some view it as a trap that limits personal freedom. This fear of being vulnerable can prevent people from entering or fully committing to relationships, leading them to remain emotionally detached or avoid intimacy altogether.

Psychologically, this fear of vulnerability is often rooted in past experiences of rejection or emotional trauma. People who have been hurt in past relationships may develop a protective mechanism that keeps them from fully investing in new ones. This defensive stance, while protective in the short term, ultimately stunts emotional growth and prevents individuals from experiencing the depth of connection that comes with real commitment. The avoidance of vulnerability leads to emotional stagnation, where individuals may continue to long for love but are unable to fully embrace the risks that come with it.

Moreover, commitment issues can create a cycle of disappointment and frustration. One or both partners may feel like they are constantly giving more than they are receiving, leading to a sense of imbalance in the relationship. The fear of vulnerability often manifests as a lack of communication or a failure to express emotional needs, leaving both individuals feeling neglected or misunderstood. Over time, this lack of emotional exchange erodes trust and respect, two key components of a healthy relationship.

In some cases, commitment issues can lead to self-sabotage. The fear of being hurt may cause individuals to engage in behaviours that undermine their relationships, such as cheating, withdrawing emotionally, or avoiding discussions about the future. This creates a self-fulfilling prophecy, where the individual's fear of rejection leads them to act in ways that ultimately push their partner away. The inability to confront these issues head-on only reinforces the belief that commitment is dangerous, leaving the individual trapped in a cycle of emotional isolation.

14. Cheating: The Betrayal of Trust and Respect

Cheating, whether emotional or physical, has become an unfortunate but common feature in modern relationships. This betrayal of trust is often seen because of dissatisfaction or a failure to communicate needs within the relationship. In the context of situation ships, where there is no clear commitment, cheating may be more likely due to the lack of boundaries or expectations. However, in more traditional relationships, cheating is a blatant disregard for the trust and respect that should form the foundation of the partnership.

The psychological effects of cheating are devastating for both the victim and the perpetrator. For the person cheated on, the emotional trauma can lead to a loss of self-esteem, anxiety, and depression. Trust is one of the most critical components of any relationship, and once it is broken, it can be extremely difficult to rebuild. The victim may experience feelings of worthlessness or self-doubt, questioning their attractiveness, their ability to maintain a relationship, or their worthiness of love. These emotional scars often linger long after the relationship ends, making it difficult to trust others in future connections.

For the person who cheats, there is often a complex web of emotions that include guilt, shame, and a sense of internal conflict. While some may justify their actions by citing dissatisfaction in the relationship or the thrill of seeking something new, the reality is that cheating often stems from deeper psychological issues such as fear of intimacy, unresolved trauma, or a lack of emotional maturity. The act of cheating may provide temporary relief or excitement but ultimately leaves the individual with unresolved guilt and a sense of disconnection from both their partner and them.

The betrayal caused by cheating also has lasting consequences on how individuals perceive love and respect. For many, the experience of being cheated on can make it harder to trust others or to view relationships as inherently stable and fulfilling. It fosters a cynical outlook on love, where commitment becomes less about loyalty and more about personal convenience. This shift in perspective leads to a generation where loyalty is undervalued and where respect for one's partner is seen as optional rather than essential.

15. The Disconnect Between Words and Actions

In modern relationships, there is often a disconnect between what people say and what they do. This is particularly evident in the way individuals express affection or commitment but fail to follow through with actions that demonstrate these sentiments. Words like "I love you," "I care about you," or "I'm committed to you" are thrown around without the corresponding actions that prove their sincerity. This inconsistency between words and actions leads to confusion, frustration, and ultimately a lack of trust in the relationship.

The psychological impact of this disconnect is profound. When words do not align with actions, it creates cognitive dissonance—the psychological discomfort that arises from holding conflicting beliefs or attitudes. The person who is on the receiving end of these empty promises may begin to feel invalidated or neglected, as their partner's words don't match their behaviour. This dissonance can lead to frustration, insecurity, and a growing sense of disillusionment with the relationship. Over time, the emotional toll of being promised one thing but experiencing another can erode the bond between partners.

This disconnect also undermines the sense of security and stability that is necessary for a healthy relationship. When individuals repeatedly fail to act in accordance with their promises, it leads to an erosion of trust. The partner who is on the receiving end of these broken promises may begin to question the authenticity of their partner's feelings and the future of the relationship. The uncertainty created by this disconnect can lead to anxiety, as both parties are left wondering whether they can rely on each other.

Finally, the disconnect between words and actions can lead to emotional exhaustion. When individuals are constantly being let down by their partner's lack of follow-through, it can feel like an emotional burden. The person who is trying to maintain the relationship may become tired of offering emotional support without receiving the same in return. This imbalance can lead to resentment and a sense of emotional depletion, making it difficult to sustain the relationship in the long run.

16. The Cycle of Unfulfilled Expectations

One of the most damaging aspects of modern relationships is the cycle of unfulfilled expectations. People enter relationships with high hopes and the expectation that their emotional, physical, and social needs will be met by their partner. However, when those expectations are not met, disappointment and resentment begin to build. This cycle often becomes self-perpetuating, as unfulfilled expectations lead to emotional withdrawal, lack of communication, and eventually the disintegration of the relationship.

Psychologically, the cycle of unfulfilled expectations can cause deep emotional pain. When individuals feel that their needs are consistently ignored or unmet, they begin to question their worth and their ability to find true happiness. The constant let down creates an underlying sense of dissatisfaction, which can negatively affect one's mental health and self-esteem. As the cycle continues, the relationship becomes less about mutual support and more about frustration, leading to a breakdown of the emotional bond.

Moreover, unfulfilled expectations often lead to resentment, which can further complicate the relationship dynamic. When one partner feels neglected or disrespected, they may become defensive or emotionally distant, creating a barrier to honest communication. The other partner, in turn, may feel misunderstood or unappreciated, perpetuating the cycle of unfulfilled expectations. Over time, the build-up of these negative emotions can make it difficult to see the relationship in a positive light, leading to the eventual collapse of the bond.

Lastly, the failure to meet each other's expectations can lead to a sense of powerlessness in both individuals. They may feel as though they are putting in effort but not receiving anything in return, leading to feelings of frustration and helplessness. This emotional drain can prevent the individuals from recognising the value of their relationship, even if it has potential. As the cycle of unmet expectations continues, it becomes harder for either partner to remain hopeful about the future, and the relationship may slowly fade away.

17. Lack of Accountability in Relationships

In the age of situation ships and casual relationships, accountability has become a rare quality. Many individuals no longer take responsibility for their actions, particularly when it comes to how they treat their partners. The reluctance to engage in honest communication about one's needs, mistakes, or feelings creates an environment where blame-shifting becomes the norm. When people fail to hold themselves accountable in relationships, it leads to a breakdown in trust and emotional connection.

Psychologically, a lack of accountability can cause significant distress for both individuals involved. The partner who is on the receiving end of blame-shifting or denial of responsibility may feel powerless, invalidated, or taken for granted. This creates feelings of helplessness, as the person cannot trust that their concerns will be acknowledged or respected. Over time, this emotional neglect builds resentment, eroding the foundation of mutual respect necessary for a healthy relationship. When one or both parties refuse to take responsibility for their actions, it leads to unresolved conflicts and a lack of growth in the relationship.

For the person who avoids accountability, the psychological impact is equally damaging. Without acknowledging their faults or mistakes, they may never develop the emotional maturity needed to grow as an individual or in future relationships. This avoidance of responsibility can prevent personal growth, perpetuating toxic behaviours such as emotional manipulation, lying, or gaslighting. By failing to take ownership of their actions, individuals miss out on the opportunity to learn from their mistakes and build healthier relationship patterns in the future.

The absence of accountability also perpetuates a culture of emotional neglect. Partners may begin to feel like their emotional needs are irrelevant, as their concerns are dismissed or ignored. This creates an emotional disconnection where one partner feels as if they are giving without receiving in return. In the long term, this imbalance leads to emotional burnout and an increasing sense of dissatisfaction with the relationship. Ultimately, the failure to be accountable is a silent but powerful force that can destroy the foundation of respect and trust in a partnership.

18. Emotional Unavailability: The Fear of Intimacy

Emotional unavailability is a significant issue in modern relationships, especially among those who have experienced trauma, rejection, or a general fear of vulnerability. Individuals who are emotionally unavailable may engage in relationships but avoid deep emotional engagement, preferring to keep things surface-level. This avoidance of intimacy can be a defence mechanism against the fear of getting hurt or rejected. Over time, emotional unavailability creates a barrier to forming meaningful and authentic connections.

Psychologically, emotional unavailability often stems from a fear of being vulnerable. Past emotional wounds—such as betrayal or neglect—can make individuals hesitant to open up fully to others. The fear of emotional pain leads to self-protection, resulting in behaviours like withdrawing, shutting down, or avoiding emotionally intense conversations. While this self-defence mechanism may provide temporary relief, it ultimately leaves the person feeling disconnected and isolated. Emotional unavailability can prevent individuals from experiencing the depth of love, affection, and understanding that comes with vulnerability and emotional intimacy.

Furthermore, emotional unavailability can lead to chronic loneliness, even within a relationship. When one person is emotionally closed off, the other may feel as though they are giving more than they are receiving. This imbalance creates an emotional divide that prevents the relationship from flourishing. Over time, the person who is emotionally available may become frustrated or hurt by their partner's lack of engagement, leading to feelings of neglect, confusion, and disappointment. The inability to connect on an emotional level leaves both parties unfulfilled and can ultimately lead to the dissolution of the relationship.

In terms of personal growth, emotional unavailability stunts emotional development. Individuals who avoid emotional intimacy may struggle with forming healthy, lasting relationships in the future. The lack of emotional depth can also cause individuals to become numb or disconnected from their own feelings, making it harder to engage in meaningful self-reflection or emotional healing. Without the ability to confront and process their emotions, individuals may carry unresolved issues into future relationships, perpetuating a cycle of emotional unavailability.

19. The Lack of Empathy and Compassion in Relationships

In modern relationships, there is an increasing lack of empathy and compassion, two qualities that are essential for fostering emotional connection and mutual respect. The fast-paced nature of today's world, combined with the rise of individualism, has led many people to focus on their own needs and desires, often at the expense of understanding or caring for their partner's feelings. This lack of empathy undermines the emotional intimacy necessary for building strong, supportive relationships.

Psychologically, a lack of empathy can cause emotional isolation. When one partner fails to empathise with the other's struggles, fears, or needs, it creates a sense of being misunderstood or neglected. The individual who is not being heard may feel invalidated, leading to frustration, sadness, and a sense of disconnection. This emotional distance can erode the trust and intimacy that are required for a healthy relationship. Without empathy, there is no genuine understanding or support, and the relationship becomes an environment of emotional neglect.

Additionally, the absence of compassion can lead to emotional burnout. When individuals fail to offer compassion to their partner, it creates a one-sided relationship where one person does all the emotional work while the other remains emotionally detached. This imbalance causes frustration and resentment, as one partner feels overburdened while the other remains emotionally distant. Over time, this lack of compassion can cause significant strain on the relationship, making it increasingly difficult to maintain a healthy and loving bond.

Lastly, the inability to show empathy and compassion can result in emotional detachment and avoidance of difficult conversations. Couples who lack empathy may avoid addressing their problems or engaging in difficult discussions because they feel no obligation to understand each other's perspective. This avoidance of emotional labour leads to unresolved conflicts and a growing emotional divide, which ultimately diminishes the quality of the relationship. In the absence of empathy and compassion, relationships lose their ability to nurture and grow, leaving individuals emotionally depleted and disconnected from each other.

Solutions

1. Emphasise Clear Communication and Boundaries

One of the foundational solutions for improving relationships and restoring mutual respect is the emphasis on clear communication and setting boundaries. Open, honest, and direct conversations about expectations, emotional needs, and future goals are vital. Partners should feel comfortable expressing their desires, fears, and vulnerabilities without fear of judgment or rejection. Communication is not just about words—it's about listening with empathy and understanding the other person's perspective.

By establishing clear boundaries from the outset, both partners can avoid misunderstandings or assumptions about the relationship's nature. This can help prevent situation ships from evolving into emotionally confusing or draining experiences. Setting and respecting boundaries encourages mutual respect and shows each person that their emotional well-being is valued. When boundaries are violated, addressing the issue immediately can prevent the erosion of trust and respect.

2. Prioritise Emotional Availability and Vulnerability

To combat emotional unavailability, individuals must consciously try to become more emotionally open and available to their partners. This involves allowing oneself to be vulnerable, sharing feelings, and being receptive to emotional intimacy. Vulnerability is not a weakness but a strength that builds trust and connection. Individuals need to be willing to confront their fears of rejection and embrace the risks of emotional openness.

Fostering emotional vulnerability in relationships requires ongoing self-reflection and healing. Past traumas or fears of intimacy must be acknowledged and addressed with compassion, either through self-work or therapy. Emotional availability helps deepen connections and allows both partners to experience the full spectrum of intimacy and trust. It also helps break the cycle of emotional detachment, fostering a healthy and nurturing relationship.

3. Commit to Personal Growth and Self-Reflection

Commitment issues can often be traced back to personal insecurities or fears of emotional dependency. Overcoming commitment issues requires a commitment to personal growth, which includes working on self-esteem, emotional intelligence, and conflict-resolution skills. Individuals must reflect on past relationships and explore the underlying reasons behind their fear of commitment. This may involve confronting past emotional wounds and learning healthier ways of engaging with others.

Commitment also requires the ability to trust and be trusted. Therapy, journaling, or open discussions with a partner can help individuals work through their issues and redefine their perceptions of love and connection. By committing to personal growth, individuals can create a healthier sense of self, which leads to stronger, more fulfilling relationships built on mutual respect and trust.

4. Build Accountability and Responsibility

Restoring accountability in relationships is crucial for repairing the damage done by situation ships and emotional detachment. Partners should hold each other accountable for their actions, taking responsibility for their mistakes and learning from them. This involves confronting uncomfortable emotions and having difficult conversations about what went wrong, without deflecting blame or avoiding responsibility. Taking ownership of one's actions promotes emotional maturity and strengthens the foundation of respect within the relationship.

Accountability also requires acknowledging the impact of one's behaviour on the other person's well-being. By developing a deeper awareness of how actions affect others, individuals can begin to make more conscious choices that foster respect and mutual support. Partners who are willing to be held accountable and take responsibility for their actions are more likely to create lasting, healthy relationships.

5. Re-establish Respect for Boundaries and Expectations

The absence of respect for each other's boundaries and emotional needs can lead to frustration, resentment, and eventual relationship breakdown. Partners need to re-establish mutual respect by clearly defining and respecting personal boundaries. This includes respecting emotional, physical, and mental limits, and understanding when to give each other space. Boundaries are not a sign of emotional distance but a necessary framework for healthy interaction.

For boundaries to be respected, individuals must also respect each other's autonomy and independence. Allowing each person, the freedom to maintain their individuality while being part of the relationship strengthens the partnership.

Re-establishing boundaries requires ongoing dialogue, a willingness to compromise, and a commitment to honouring each other's emotional safety.

6. Foster Healthy Dependency, Not Co-dependency

A healthy relationship requires a balance of dependency, where both individuals rely on each other for emotional support and connection. However, this dependency should not turn into co-dependency, where one person's happiness is entirely dependent on the other. Both partners must maintain their sense of self while being emotionally available and supportive for each other.

Encouraging a healthy level of interdependence involves creating a space where both individuals feel comfortable leaning on one another while also nurturing their independence. This balance promotes self-growth and emotional resilience, making the relationship stronger and more sustainable. Healthy dependency fosters a sense of partnership and collaboration, allowing both individuals to thrive individually and as a couple.

7. Invest in Self-Care and Emotional Well-being

To build healthy, respectful relationships, individuals must first prioritise their own emotional health. This includes engaging in self-care practices, cultivating self-awareness, and seeking support when needed. When people are emotionally well, they are more capable of offering love and respect to others. Additionally, self-care ensures that individuals can manage the emotional ups and downs of a relationship without relying solely on their partner for validation.

Self-care also plays a vital role in preventing unhealthy patterns such as emotional unavailability or co-dependency. When individuals nurture their mental and emotional health, they are better equipped to show up as emotionally present and supportive partners. Regularly taking time for self-reflection and personal growth helps individuals maintain emotional balance and enhances their ability to contribute positively to a relationship.

8. Normalise Healthy Emotional Expression

One of the ways to rebuild respect in relationships is by normalising healthy emotional expression. This involves creating a space where both partners feel safe to express their emotions without fear of judgment or ridicule. Emotional expression should be seen as a vital part of communication, not as a weakness. When both partners are open about their feelings—whether it's love, frustration, or sadness—it creates an environment of trust and transparency.

Normalising emotional expression also involves learning how to communicate difficult emotions constructively. This includes avoiding blame, being vulnerable, and actively listening to each other's perspectives. When individuals express their feelings with empathy and understanding, it strengthens the bond between them and fosters a deeper connection. Healthy emotional expression allows for greater intimacy and promotes respect for one another's emotional worlds.

9. Rebuild Trust Through Small Acts of Respect

Trust is often the hardest thing to rebuild after it has been broken, but it can be restored through consistent actions of respect and care. Rebuilding trust requires both partners to demonstrate reliability, honesty, and accountability in every aspect of their relationship. Small acts of respect—such as being on time, honouring promises, or expressing appreciation—build trust over time and reaffirm the commitment to a healthy relationship.

Each small act of respect demonstrates a genuine desire to value and care for the other person. Over time, these acts accumulate and create a foundation of trust that can weather larger challenges. Rebuilding trust is a process that requires patience, but when both partners are committed to showing respect through their actions, trust can be renewed.

10. Practice Compassion and Empathy

Finally, practicing compassion and empathy is key to restoring respect and emotional connection in relationships. Understanding and sharing in the feelings of others, especially during difficult times, helps to foster a deeper sense of connection. When partners approach each other with empathy, they are more likely to listen without judgment and respond with kindness and care.

Compassion is essential for healing emotional wounds caused by disrespect or neglect. It allows both partners to forgive each other for mistakes and approach the relationship with understanding rather than blame. Practicing compassion and empathy leads to more harmonious relationships, where both partners feel seen, heard, and supported. Compassionate responses create a safe emotional environment that nurtures respect and love.

By implementing these solutions, individuals can restore the emotional health, respect, and trust that have been lost in modern relationship dynamics. It requires consistent effort, self-awareness, and a commitment to personal and relational growth, but the results will be more fulfilling, authentic, and lasting connections.

The long-term emotional effects of situationships often go unnoticed until they reach a breaking point. Many individuals who engage in these types of relationships find their self-worth tied to the fluctuating dynamics of the connection. When the other person is distant or emotionally unavailable, feelings of inadequacy and insecurity begin to emerge.

This constant emotional rollercoaster, where one moment everything seems fine and the next, there is silence or indifference, leads to a loss of self-esteem. Over time, individuals in situationships begin to question their value, believing that they are not worthy of a committed relationship or that they must "prove" their worth.

Moving Forward: Reclaiming Respect and Connection

To break free from the cycle of situationships, it's essential to redefine what respect looks like in today's relationships. It's about returning to the basics—open communication, mutual care, and honouring each other's emotional needs. Respect isn't just about politeness or surface-level actions; it's about creating an environment where both individuals can thrive emotionally, without the fear of exploitation or neglect.

By reclaiming respect, we can create relationships that are grounded in trust, honesty, and mutual care—relationships that transcend the transactional nature of situationships and move toward deeper, more meaningful connections.

Chapter 9

Modesty, Not Mediocrity

In a world where excess is often celebrated, modesty can sometimes be misunderstood as mediocrity. Society has conditioned us to believe that to stand out, we must flaunt our achievements, our wealth, and our status. The louder we speak, the more attention we receive, and in this noise, modesty can be viewed as a weakness, or worse, a lack of ambition.

However, modesty is not about fading into the background or diminishing one's value. It is about understanding the deeper, more meaningful aspects of one's character and presenting them in a way that is authentic, grounded, and sincere. Modesty is not about shrinking or hiding—it is about knowing when to step forward and when to allow others to shine. In this sense, true modesty is an act of strength, not mediocrity.

Social media has amplified the culture of self-promotion, where personal branding has become a business. The platforms we use to connect with others often double as stages for showcasing our best selves—our curated lives, flawless images, and most impressive accomplishments. The race to keep up with influencers, celebrities, and even peers can make modesty seem outdated, as if holding back or not showcasing every accomplishment diminishes your worth.

Yet, in the relentless pursuit of attention and validation, we often lose sight of what truly makes us valuable. Constant self-promotion can be exhausting and, at times, empty. The pursuit of external validation, through likes and comments, may mask an underlying lack of fulfilment. True modesty does not depend on how many followers or accolades one has.

It comes from an inner understanding of one's worth, free from the need for external recognition.

Modesty, when practiced in leadership, has the power to create environments of trust and respect. In contrast to the dominant paradigm of "alpha" leadership, which often emphasizes dominance, control, and personal achievement, modest leadership is grounded in humility, service, and collaboration.

Great leaders do not seek to elevate themselves above others. Instead, they recognize the strengths of their team and empower them to rise. They are willing to step back, share the spotlight, and ensure that others have the opportunity to succeed. This doesn't mean they lack confidence or vision—in fact, the best leaders are confident in their abilities but do not need to constantly prove it.

True leadership is about listening more than speaking, asking more than commanding, and uplifting others rather than self-promotion. This type of leadership not only fosters a healthy, supportive work culture but also inspires those around them to pursue their own ambitions with integrity and humility.

One of the core tenets of modesty is simplicity. In a world that often celebrates excess—whether it's the latest fashion, the newest gadgets, or the most expensive vacations—modesty offers an alternative. Simple living is not about deprivation but about making conscious choices to prioritize what is truly important.

In fashion, for example, simplicity can be seen in the concept of the capsule wardrobe—choosing timeless pieces that can be mixed and matched rather than constantly chasing trends. In lifestyle, it may mean prioritizing experiences over material possessions, focusing on relationships over social media, or choosing quiet time over constant busyness.

Simplicity, when embraced with intentionality, leads to greater clarity and peace. It removes the distractions and excess that clutter our lives, allowing us to focus on what truly brings joy and fulfilment. By embracing modesty and simplicity, we cultivate a life of purpose, not one defined by the pursuit of things or external validation In today's world, where everyone's life is broadcasted for all to see, practicing modesty may seem like an act of rebellion. But in the digital age, modesty is more important than ever. With the constant bombardment of curated images on social media, it is easy to fall into the trap of comparison and competition. People often measure their worth by how much attention they receive or how "perfect" their life appears to others.

Modesty offers a counter-narrative. It reminds us that we do not need to broadcast every achievement, every success, or every aspect of our personal lives to be valuable. It encourages us to embrace authenticity, to be content with who we are, and to resist the pressure to present a flawless, curated version of ourselves.

By practicing modesty in the digital age, we can reclaim our power from the noise of social media. We can focus on what matters to us, not what others think of us. This shift in mindset allows us to live more peacefully, more authentically, and more connected to our true selves.

1. Redefining Modesty in the Modern World

Modesty has long been associated with physical appearance, often focusing on covering up or minimising one's presence. However, in today's world, modesty transcends the superficial and delves into the realm of self-expression and humility. It's not about hiding who you are but rather embodying a sense of balance and self-respect. Modesty in behaviour can manifest as being respectful of others' space and acknowledging one's own limitations, which makes for more harmonious interactions.

As society becomes more focused on individualism and self-promotion, the concept of modesty is often overlooked in favour of attention-seeking behaviours. Modesty encourages the recognition that we are not the centre of the universe, yet we have value in our unique contributions. It fosters a sense of collective well-being, where people respect each other's boundaries and ideas rather than constantly trying to outshine one another.

Redefining modesty in this way invites a more inclusive society, where the focus shifts from one-upping others to supporting and valuing their presence. Embracing modesty allows individuals to shine without overshadowing others, fostering a more collaborative and empathetic environment. This shift requires rethinking success, moving beyond mere recognition to a deeper understanding of fulfilment and impact.

Solution: Encourage individuals to find balance in their expressions of identity that reflect both their values and personality without excess.

2. The Power of Humility in Personal Growth

Humility is often misunderstood as weakness or a lack of self-esteem, but in truth, it is a powerful trait that fosters personal growth. Humility allows us to remain open to feedback and to admit when we don't know something. This openness is essential for learning and evolving. A humble individual does not see themselves as above others but rather as a part of a collective effort, which enables them to absorb knowledge and experiences that might otherwise be overlooked.

Furthermore, humility prevents the stagnation that comes with arrogance. When we believe we know everything, there is no room for improvement. Humility, on the other hand, makes us more approachable and receptive, encouraging deeper connections with others and facilitating collaborative growth. It also promotes emotional intelligence, as humble people are often more empathetic and understanding of others' needs and perspectives.

Being humble does not mean diminishing one's worth or capabilities. It means recognising that we are all continuously evolving, and that the journey is more important than the destination. Humility enables us to enjoy the process of learning and developing, rather than focusing solely on the accolades we might receive. This approach leads to sustainable personal growth, as it nurtures both self-improvement and meaningful relationships.

Solution: Emphasise continuous learning and embracing feedback without taking it as criticism.

3. Authenticity Over Perfection

In a world that often prioritises polished, idealised versions of people and experiences, authenticity has become a rare and valuable commodity. People are constantly striving to fit a mold of perfection—whether in their appearance, careers, or personal lives. However, the pursuit of perfection can lead to a sense of inadequacy, as perfection is an illusion. Authenticity, on the other hand, allows individuals to embrace their true selves, flaws and all, leading to a deeper sense of contentment and confidence.

When we focus on being authentic, we remove the pressure to conform to external standards and instead place value on our unique qualities. Authenticity encourages self-reflection, enabling us to align our actions with our core values. It fosters a sense of inner peace because we are no longer constantly battling against an idealised version of ourselves. By choosing authenticity over perfection, we give ourselves permission to be imperfect, which is ultimately what makes us real and relatable.

Being authentic also helps build stronger, more genuine relationships. When we allow ourselves to be vulnerable and honest, we invite others to do the same. This mutual openness creates a foundation of trust and respect, which is far more meaningful than any superficial perfection could ever provide. Authenticity attracts the right people and experiences into our lives—those that are rooted in sincerity and truth.

Solution: Promote self-acceptance and encourage individuals to embrace their flaws as part of their uniqueness.

4. Modesty as a Strength in a Materialistic Society

In a world driven by consumerism and the constant need for validation through material possessions, modesty stands as a counterbalance. The modern era often equates success with the accumulation of wealth and status symbols, leading many to chase after the next big purchase or trend. However, modesty challenges this notion by placing value on intangible qualities such as integrity, kindness, and empathy, rather than material gain.

The strength of modesty lies in its ability to promote long-term happiness rather than short-term gratification. People who practice modesty tend to prioritise experiences and relationships over material goods, fostering a sense of contentment and fulfilment that doesn't rely on external factors. They are more likely to appreciate the simple joys in life, like spending time with loved ones or enjoying nature, rather than seeking out the latest trend or luxury item.

Moreover, modesty in a materialistic society can also be a form of rebellion against the pressures of consumer culture. It invites individuals to step away from the constant cycle of comparison and competition, focusing instead on what truly matters to them. By rejecting the idea that happiness comes from external possessions, those who embrace modesty can lead more authentic and fulfilling lives.

Solution: Cultivate mindfulness about consumption, focusing on quality over quantity in all aspects of life.

5. The Role of Self-Awareness in Building True Confidence

Self-awareness is the cornerstone of genuine confidence. Unlike the kind of confidence that comes from external validation or temporary achievements, self-awareness enables individuals to develop an inner sense of security. When we understand our strengths, weaknesses, and values, we no longer need to seek approval from others, as our confidence is rooted in who we are, not in what we can do for others.

Self-awareness also helps us navigate challenges with a clear mind. When we are aware of our emotional triggers and behavioural patterns, we can make more informed decisions and respond to situations with composure and integrity. It allows us to handle criticism constructively and learn from our mistakes without feeling threatened or insecure. This type of confidence is resilient, as it is not dependent on external factors or fleeting successes.

Furthermore, self-awareness encourages personal growth. It prompts individuals to continuously reflect on their actions and thoughts, seeking ways to improve and align with their true selves. By cultivating self-awareness, we develop a confidence that is sustainable and rooted in authenticity. This kind of confidence attracts opportunities and relationships that are aligned with our values and aspirations.

Solution: Practice regular self-reflection through journaling or meditation to deepen self-awareness.

6. Balancing Ambition with Humility

Ambition is often seen as a key driver of success, but when coupled with humility, it becomes a force for good. Ambition without humility can lead to arrogance and self-centred behaviour, where the focus is solely on personal gain and recognition. However, when ambition is tempered with humility, it encourages individuals to pursue their goals with a sense of purpose and integrity, rather than ego-driven motives.

Balancing ambition with humility means recognising that success is not solely the result of personal effort, but also of the support and contributions of others. Humble individuals acknowledge the roles that mentors, colleagues, and even setbacks have played in their journey. This mindset not only fosters gratitude but also creates a sense of community, where success is shared rather than hoarded.

Furthermore, humility keeps ambition in check by reminding individuals of their purpose and values. It prevents them from losing sight of what truly matters in their pursuit of success. By prioritising meaningful goals and striving for personal excellence rather than external validation, individuals can achieve success that is both rewarding and fulfilling, creating a legacy that is rooted in positive impact.

Solution: Set realistic, meaningful goals that are aligned with your core values, not just status or wealth.

7. Cultivating Humility in Leadership

Leadership often comes with power, but true leadership is defined by humility. A humble leader recognises that their position is a privilege and responsibility, not a platform for self-aggrandisement. They approach leadership with the mindset that their role is to serve others, not to dominate or control. This humility creates an environment of trust and respect, where employees, teammates, or followers feel valued and empowered.

A humble leader also prioritises collaboration over competition, encouraging team members to share their ideas and talents freely. By acknowledging the contributions of others and giving credit where it's due, humble leaders build strong, loyal teams. This type of leadership fosters a positive culture where individuals are motivated by the collective success rather than personal gain. It encourages open communication and transparency, which are essential for long-term success.

Additionally, humility in leadership means being willing to admit mistakes and learn from them. A leader who can own their errors demonstrates vulnerability, which builds trust with their team. By modelling this behaviour, they set an example for others to follow, showing that mistakes are opportunities for growth rather than reasons for shame. Humble leadership creates a cycle of continuous improvement, where everyone is encouraged to strive for betterment.

Solution: Leaders should focus on empowering others and sharing successes, rather than taking sole credit.

8. Why Modesty Helps Foster Better Relationships

Modesty in behaviour is foundational to fostering meaningful and lasting relationships. Whether in personal or professional interactions, modesty promotes respect, kindness, and consideration for others. A modest individual doesn't need to dominate conversations or seek the spotlight; they make space for others to share their thoughts, creating an environment of mutual respect. This kind of openness fosters stronger bonds, as individuals feel valued and heard.

Modesty also helps prevent the creation of toxic dynamics in relationships, where one party seeks to assert dominance or control. By adopting a humble approach, we learn to appreciate others for who they are and not for what they can do for us. This creates a healthy, balanced relationship where both parties are equally invested in each other's well-being. Modesty fosters a sense of equality, reducing power imbalances and ensuring that both voices are heard and respected.

Moreover, modesty in relationships encourages emotional vulnerability, which is crucial for building deep connections. When we let go of the need to impress or control, we can open up and show our true selves. This honesty strengthens trust and deepens emotional intimacy, making relationships more fulfilling. In a world that often prioritises superficial connections, modesty acts as a reminder of the importance of genuine, meaningful interaction.

Solution: Practice active listening and value others' perspectives without dominating conversations.

9. The Dangers of Overconfidence

While confidence is a valuable trait, overconfidence can be detrimental to both personal growth and relationships. Overconfident individuals often believe they have all the answers, leading them to dismiss the input or concerns of others. This arrogance can create friction in relationships, as others may feel undervalued or unheard. Overconfidence also leads to poor decision-making, as individuals may fail to consider alternative perspectives or recognise their own limitations.

In the workplace, overconfidence can result in missed opportunities for collaboration and innovation. Those who believe they know it all are less likely to seek feedback or share credit with others, which stifles creativity and growth. This attitude can also alienate colleagues, as it fosters a competitive environment rather than one of cooperation. Overconfidence often leads to failure, as the refusal to acknowledge mistakes prevents learning and improvement.

On a personal level, overconfidence can lead to unrealistic expectations, resulting in disappointment when outcomes don't align with one's inflated self-assessment. This can lead to frustration and a lack of self-awareness, making it harder to grow emotionally and intellectually. Modesty offers a safeguard against overconfidence by encouraging individuals to acknowledge their limitations, embrace feedback, and continuously strive for improvement.

Solution: Focus on growth over pride, being open to improvement and recognising the limitations of one's own knowledge.

10. Modesty in the Digital Age

The digital age has brought about new challenges in how we present ourselves to the world. Social media platforms encourage the curation of perfect, filtered images and highlight reels of success, creating unrealistic standards for how we should look and live. Modesty, however, offers a counterpoint to this hyper-curated world. Instead of focusing on constructing an idealised version of ourselves, modesty invites us to share our true, unfiltered selves, flaws, and all.

In the digital age, modesty is about using technology to connect authentically with others, rather than seeking external validation. Rather than posting for likes or followers, modesty encourages sharing content that reflects your genuine interests, values, and experiences. This creates a more meaningful online presence, one that attracts individuals who appreciate authenticity over superficial perfection. In turn, this can lead to more supportive and uplifting online communities.

Moreover, modesty in the digital world can help mitigate the harmful effects of comparison culture. Social media often promotes a sense of inadequacy by highlighting only the best parts of people's lives. Modesty offers a reminder that everyone has struggles and imperfections, and that these should be acknowledged and embraced. By shifting the focus from constant comparison to self-acceptance, we can create a healthier digital environment for ourselves and others.

Solution: Prioritise authentic self-expression online, avoiding comparisons to curated online personas.

The journey toward embracing modesty is not about rejecting success, ambition, or hard work. It is about finding a balance that honours our worth without inflating our egos or seeking constant approval from others. Modesty is not a rejection of greatness but a recognition that greatness can exist without the need for loud, attention-seeking behaviour.

As we embrace modesty, we reclaim our sense of peace, purpose, and authenticity. We move away from the need for validation and instead focus on cultivating a life that is rich in meaning, fulfilment, and joy. By choosing modesty, we reject mediocrity and embrace a life of intentionality and depth—one that leaves a lasting impact on the world around us.

Chapter 10

The Mirror of Self-Reflection

The Mirror of Self-Reflection

1. **Introduction to Self-Reflection** As we navigate through life, we often find ourselves swept up in the hustle of daily routines, chasing after goals and adhering to external expectations. But amidst the noise, we seldom pause to examine our own lives—our actions, decisions, and desires. The "Mirror of Self-Reflection" is a metaphorical tool that invites us to take a moment to truly look at ourselves, to understand not only who we are but also who we aspire to become. It encourages introspection, allowing us to assess whether our current path aligns with our true values and purpose.

Self-reflection is a powerful tool for personal growth. It offers an opportunity to pause, evaluate, and realign our lives in a more intentional direction. In our busy world, where distractions are abundant, it can be difficult to slow down and turn our gaze inward. Yet, by doing so, we can rediscover our core values and remember what truly matters to us. It's a crucial step toward cultivating self-awareness and personal integrity.

By engaging with self-reflection, we allow ourselves the chance to detach from the chaos of the world and reconnect with our inner selves. This practice can be transformative, enabling us to let go of outdated beliefs or habits and step forward with clarity and purpose. When we look into the mirror of self-reflection, we don't just see the surface; we are called to look deeper, to explore the motivations behind our actions, and to confront the truth about ourselves.

2. The Importance of Honesty with Us Honesty with oneself is the cornerstone of self-reflection. Without it, the process becomes futile, as we risk living in denial of our true feelings and desires. It is easy to construct a facade, convincing ourselves that we are content, successful, or fulfilled when we may feel lost, disconnected, or unfulfilled. The mirror of self-reflection challenges us to face these uncomfortable truths.

True self-reflection requires a willingness to be brutally honest about our flaws, our failures, and our successes. It involves acknowledging areas of our lives where we may have fallen short or where our actions have not aligned with our values. This honesty isn't about self-criticism but about self-acceptance. Recognising our imperfections allows us to embrace them and work toward improving them. Only by being honest with ourselves can we identify where change is needed and take proactive steps toward it.

It is also essential to recognise that being honest with ourselves does not mean punishing ourselves for past mistakes. Rather, it's about acknowledging the present moment and using it as a foundation for growth. The mirror of self-reflection does not show us a distorted image; it presents an accurate picture, one that allows us to build upon the truth and move forward in a more authentic way.

3. Facing Our Fears One of the most difficult aspects of self-reflection is confronting our fears. Fear often holds us back from pursuing our true potential and keeps us stuck in comfort zones that no longer serve us. Whether it is fear of failure, fear of judgment, or fear of the unknown, these fears can cloud our judgment and prevent us from making empowered choices.

However, the mirror of self-reflection reveals these fears for what they are: obstacles that we have the power to overcome. When we look deeply into ourselves, we can recognise the irrationality behind many of our fears and begin to challenge them. Understanding that fear is often a product of past experiences or societal conditioning helps us break free from its hold. In this space, we gain the courage to take risks, make bold decisions, and embrace uncertainty as a necessary part of growth.

Self-reflection teaches us that fear is not something to be avoided but something to be understood and integrated into our lives. Instead of allowing fear to control us, we can choose to face it with courage and self-compassion. It's through this process that we begin to move past our limitations and toward the freedom of living authentically and confidently.

4. Recognising Our Values Self-reflection is a powerful tool for rediscovering our core values. In a world where external pressures often dictate our choices, it's easy to lose sight of what we truly value. The mirror of self-reflection helps us reconnect with our intrinsic beliefs, passions, and motivations, giving us the clarity needed to make decisions that are aligned with our authentic selves.

Our values are the foundation of who we are. They influence our relationships, our career choices, and our approach to life. Without a clear understanding of our values, we may find ourselves pursuing goals that don't bring us fulfilment or engaging in activities that conflict with our sense of integrity. By reflecting on what truly matters to us, we can recalibrate our actions and focus on what is most important.

Through self-reflection, we can identify any discrepancies between our values and our current actions. This awareness enables us to make conscious choices that honour our values, leading to a life that feels more meaningful and fulfilling. Whether it's prioritising family, creativity, personal growth, or service to others, recognising and living by our values allows us to lead a life of purpose and authenticity.

5. Letting Go of the Past The past can weigh heavily on us, influencing the way we think, feel, and act in the present. Past mistakes, regrets, or unhealed wounds can often prevent us from moving forward. The mirror of self-reflection encourages us to acknowledge the past, but it also challenges us to release it. Letting go of the past is not about forgetting; it's about releasing the emotional grip it has on us.

Self-reflection provides an opportunity to examine our past experiences with a sense of detachment, allowing us to learn from them without letting them define us. When we reflect on past mistakes, we can gain insights that help us make better choices in the future. However, we must also recognize that we cannot change what has already happened. The power lies in how we choose to move forward from those experiences, with wisdom, resilience, and grace.

Letting go of the past involves forgiveness—both of ourselves and others. It's about choosing peace over resentment and growth over stagnation. By releasing old grudges, regrets, and self-blame, we free ourselves to embrace the present and the future with a renewed sense of hope and possibility.

6. Reconnecting with Our Purpose Self-reflection is a powerful way to reconnect with our purpose. In the midst of daily distractions, it is easy to lose sight of why we do what we do. The mirror of self-reflection allows us to step back and evaluate whether our current path aligns with our deeper sense of purpose. Purpose is the guiding force that gives our lives meaning, and when we feel disconnected from it, we may experience a sense of emptiness or dissatisfaction.

Through reflection, we can rediscover what truly drives us. This may involve revisiting long-forgotten dreams, passions, or goals that once brought us joy. It's about tuning into what excites and motivates us, beyond external expectations or societal pressures. Our purpose is unique to us, and only through self-reflection can we uncover the clarity needed to align our actions with it.

Reconnecting with our purpose also means shedding the layers of doubt and fear that may have obscured it. When we reflect deeply, we gain the courage to take bold steps toward living a life that feels authentic and fulfilling. Our purpose becomes a compass that guides us toward decisions and actions that resonate with our truest selves.

7. Embracing Change and Growth Change is inevitable, and personal growth is often uncomfortable. The mirror of self-reflection helps us accept that change is a natural part of life, and that growth requires us to step out of our comfort zones. Whether it's changing our mindset, adopting new habits, or letting go of limiting beliefs, self-reflection provides the space needed to assess where change is necessary.

Embracing change can be difficult, especially when it challenges our sense of identity or security. However, self-reflection encourages us to see change as an opportunity for growth rather than something to fear. By examining our current state with honesty and openness, we can identify areas where transformation is needed. Change becomes not something to resist, but a path to becoming the best version of ourselves.

Through self-reflection, we learn to view challenges as opportunities to evolve. Each moment of discomfort or uncertainty is a chance to grow stronger, wiser, and more aligned with our purpose. Embracing change allows us to live with intention, fostering an adaptive mindset that can handle whatever life throws our way.

8. The Power of Gratitude is a transformative practice that can radically shift our perspective on life. Self-reflection encourages us to take stock of the blessings, lessons, and experiences that have shaped us. By focusing on what we are grateful for, we develop a mindset that appreciates the present moment, rather than constantly striving for what's next. This shift in perspective helps us find joy in the here and now, fostering a deeper sense of contentment.

Gratitude also shifts our focus from scarcity to abundance. It allows us to recognise the wealth of resources, relationships, and opportunities that surround us. Self-reflection, when paired with gratitude, provides a clear lens through which we can appreciate the richness of our lives, even in times of struggle. Gratitude helps us find meaning in every experience, making us more resilient in the face of challenges.

Practicing gratitude also enhances our emotional well-being. Studies have shown that expressing gratitude can reduce stress, increase happiness, and improve overall mental health. By incorporating gratitude into our daily self-reflection practice, we create a foundation for emotional balance and well-being that sustains us through life's ups and downs.

9. Cultivating Patience Self-reflection teaches us the value of patience—not only with others but also with ourselves. In a fast-paced world that demands instant results, patience is often undervalued. However, personal growth takes time, and self-improvement is a gradual process. The mirror of self-reflection reminds us to be patient with ourselves, recognising that change and progress are not always immediate.

Patience involves trusting the process and allowing things to unfold in their own time. When we are patient, we avoid the pressure of rushing through life or forcing outcomes. Instead, we take the time to nurture our personal growth and honour the journey. Self-reflection fosters this sense of patience by encouraging us to evaluate our progress without judgment, understanding that growth happens in stages.

Cultivating patience also involves accepting that setbacks and failures are part of the process. Instead of becoming discouraged, we learn to view challenges as opportunities for learning. Through self-reflection, we gain the patience to navigate these difficulties with resilience, knowing that each step forward, no matter how small, is a step toward becoming who we are meant to be.

10. Setting Intentional Goals Self-reflection helps us set intentional goals—goals that are aligned with our values, purpose, and personal growth. Instead of setting goals based on external pressures or fleeting desires, we learn to create objectives that truly reflect our inner aspirations. The mirror of self-reflection helps us ask questions like: What do I want to achieve? Why do I want to achieve it? And how can I stay true to myself while pursuing this goal?

Intentional goals are specific, measurable, and meaningful. They provide direction and focus, helping us channel our energy toward what truly matters. By reflecting on our progress regularly, we can ensure that we remain on track, making adjustments when necessary. This intentional approach to goal-setting fosters a sense of purpose and fulfilment, ensuring that our efforts are aligned with our deeper desires.

Self-reflection also helps us identify any obstacles or fears that may be preventing us from pursuing our goals. By confronting these barriers head-on, we can devise strategies to overcome them. The process of setting and achieving intentional goals becomes not just about the destination but also about the growth we experience along the way.

11. Living with Integrity At the heart of self-reflection is the desire to live with integrity. Integrity means being true to our word, our values, and our commitments. It requires us to align our actions with our beliefs, and to act consistently, even when no one is watching. The mirror of self-reflection calls us to examine whether we are living in accordance with our principles, and if not, to make the necessary changes.

Living with integrity brings a deep sense of peace and self-respect. When our actions align with our values, we feel more confident in our choices and more at ease with ourselves. Integrity also strengthens our relationships, as others can trust that we will act honourably and consistently. The mirror of self-reflection encourages us to maintain this sense of integrity, recognising that it is foundational to living an authentic and fulfilling life.

By living with integrity, we can avoid the inner conflict that arises when we act out of alignment with our true selves. It allows us to lead lives of consistency and purpose, building trust and respect both with ourselves and with others. Integrity is the compass that guides us in making choices that reflect our highest ideals, and it is through self-reflection that we cultivate this vital quality.

12. Conclusion: Embracing the Journey Self-reflection is a lifelong journey—a continual process of growth, learning, and rediscovery. It is not something that can be achieved overnight, but a practice that evolves with time. The mirror of self-reflection invites us to pause, take stock, and evaluate our lives with honesty, courage, and compassion. Through this process, we uncover our true selves and are empowered to make choices that are aligned with our purpose and values.

As we embrace this journey of self-reflection, we become more attuned to our inner wisdom and more confident in our ability to navigate life's challenges. We learn to live with intention, embracing change and growth while staying rooted in our authentic selves. The mirror of self-reflection not only reveals who we are but also who we have the potential to become. It is through this ongoing process that we can live our lives with purpose, integrity, and fulfilment.

Conclusion

The Power of Authenticity and Purpose in a Confused World

In the ever-shifting world we inhabit today, it's easy to feel overwhelmed, disconnected, and uncertain about our place within the larger scheme of things. The bombardment of constant stimuli from technology, social media, and societal expectations leaves us questioning whether we are truly living authentically or simply conforming to the pressures and standards imposed upon us. In a world filled with noise, distractions, and fleeting trends, finding the courage to embrace our authentic selves and live with purpose has never been more crucial.

The Quest for Self-Understanding: The Journey Inward

One of the most pressing challenges of our generation is the quest for self-understanding. In an age where we are bombarded with information and told how to think, feel, and act, many of us have lost touch with who we really are at our core. We live in a society that often values external validation over internal fulfilment. We are told that success is about accumulating wealth, securing a "perfect" image on social media, and ticking off a checklist of achievements that society deems worthwhile. However, as many have discovered, these markers of success do not lead to true happiness or self-contentment.

True self-understanding comes from within. It is an inner journey—one that requires courage, introspection, and a willingness to confront both the light and dark aspects of our identity. When we embark on this path, we begin to strip away the layers of societal expectations and uncover our true selves. This self-awareness becomes the foundation upon which we can build our lives. Without this clarity, we risk being swept away by the tide of external expectations and, in the process, lose sight of what truly matters.

Understanding who we are—beyond the roles we play or the labels we wear—is an essential first step in living an authentic life. It is easy to define ourselves by what we do, what we own, or how others perceive us. Yet these external identities are not who we truly are. True self-awareness requires us to connect with the essence of our being, to listen to our inner voice, and to reflect deeply on our values, passions, and aspirations. This journey is not always easy—it requires patience, vulnerability, and the willingness to confront our fears and uncertainties. But in doing so, we reclaim our power and lay the groundwork for a life that reflects our deepest truth.

The Power of Modesty in a World Obsessed with Attention

In today's hyper-connected world, where the quest for fame, recognition, and success is ever-present, modesty can seem like an antiquated concept. We live in a time when louder voices, brighter personalities, and more extravagant displays of wealth and success are celebrated. Modesty, in comparison, can be misunderstood as weakness or inferiority. But true modesty is not about shrinking into the background or downplaying our achievements. It is about embracing humility, recognizing our worth, and understanding that we do not need to constantly seek external validation to feel fulfilled.

The rise of social media has exacerbated the need for self-promotion, turning everyday individuals into influencers, brands, and commodities. We are encouraged to curate our lives, carefully selecting which moments to share and which to hide, in a bid to shape a flawless image for the world to see. This quest for perfection and attention often leads to a cycle of dissatisfaction, as we measure our worth by the likes, comments, and attention we receive from others.

However, modesty offers an antidote to this cycle. It allows us to step back and focus on what truly matters. Rather than seeking constant recognition, we can find fulfilment in the quiet moments of personal growth, meaningful relationships, and acts of kindness. Modesty is a reflection of inner confidence—it is the understanding that our worth is not determined by how much attention we receive but by the depth of our character and the integrity with which we live. True modesty is a powerful strength. It allows us to remain grounded and focused on what truly brings joy and fulfilment in life, without the need for constant validation from external sources.

In a society that often prioritizes self-promotion and external recognition, practicing modesty can be a radical act. It challenges the prevailing narrative that success is measured by how much we can acquire, how loud we can speak, or how much attention we can garner. Instead, modesty invites us to embrace a quieter, more intentional path—one that is grounded in purpose, humility, and authenticity. Through modesty, we can reconnect with what truly matters: the inner peace that comes from living in alignment with our values, cultivating deep connections with others, and contributing meaningfully to the world.

The Journey from Overachievement to Meaningful Success

Overachievement has long been heralded as the ultimate marker of success. In a world where the "hustle culture" reigns supreme, the constant drive to do more, achieve more, and be more has become a norm. We are told that we must always be striving, always be pushing, and always be doing. But in this relentless pursuit of success, we often lose sight of what truly matters.

The culture of overachievement places immense pressure on individuals, particularly young people, to perform at a level that is unsustainable. It creates a toxic environment where burnout is seen as a badge of honour, and personal well-being is sacrificed for the sake of accomplishment. The pursuit of perfection, fuelled by external expectations and societal comparisons, leads to exhaustion, anxiety, and disillusionment.

True success, however, is not about achieving more—it is about achieving the right things. Success is not measured by how much we can accomplish but by how aligned our actions are with our values and purpose. True success is about pursuing goals that bring fulfilment, contribute to the greater good, and align with our deepest passions. It is about living authentically, honouring our boundaries, and embracing the process of growth rather than the pursuit of an idealized destination.

Ambition is important, but it must be rooted in meaning, not perfection. Rather than constantly chasing external accolades, we should focus on creating lives that reflect our true aspirations, desires, and values. True ambition is about progress, not perfection—it is about striving for continuous growth, learning from our failures, and contributing to the world in ways that resonate with our authentic selves.

The Role of Respect in Building Genuine Connections

In a world that often values surface-level interactions and instant gratification, genuine human connection has become increasingly rare. We may have thousands of online followers and "friends," but how many of these connections are truly meaningful? How many of them are rooted in mutual respect, trust, and understanding? In a society where relationships are often transactional, it is essential to reclaim the value of respect in our personal and professional lives.

Respect is the foundation of any healthy relationship. It is the understanding that each individual deserves to be valued, heard, and appreciated for who they are—not for what they can provide or how they can benefit us. True respect goes beyond politeness; it involves recognizing the inherent worth of others and treating them with dignity, regardless of their status or position.

In relationships—whether romantic, platonic, or professional—respect is essential. It is the cornerstone of trust, communication, and emotional safety. When we respect others, we create a space where they can be vulnerable, authentic, and true to themselves. We allow them to express their thoughts, feelings, and needs without fear of judgment or rejection.

Respect is also crucial in our relationship with ourselves. When we respect ourselves, we set healthy boundaries, honour our needs, and prioritize our well-being. Self-respect allows us to stand firm in our values, make decisions that align with our true desires, and reject the pressure to conform to societal expectations.

Reclaiming Our Power in an Overwhelming World

In a world that often seeks to diminish our power and worth, it is essential to reclaim our sense of agency. We are constantly told what we should want, how we should look, and who we should be. But these external pressures do not define us. Our worth is not determined by our appearance, our achievements, or our popularity. Our worth is inherent—it comes from within.

Reclaiming our power begins with rejecting the narrative that we must conform to societal standards in order to be valuable. It means stepping away from the need for external validation and embracing our own worth. It means letting go of the fear of judgment and choosing to live authentically, even if it means standing apart from the crowd.

Reclaiming our power also means embracing the journey of self-discovery and personal growth. It means reconnecting with our values, our passions, and our sense of purpose. It means setting our own standards for success and measuring our progress by our own terms, not society's. Through this process, we create lives that are meaningful, fulfilling, and true to who we are.

The journey to reclaiming our power is not always easy. There will be setbacks, challenges, and moments of doubt. But by embracing authenticity, modesty, and purpose, we can navigate these obstacles with resilience and grace. We can trust that, no matter how winding the road may be, we are on the path that is meant for us.

Final Thoughts: A Life Lived with Purpose

The road to fulfilment is not a race—it is a journey. It is a process of self-discovery, growth, and transformation that requires patience, resilience, and self-compassion. Along the way, we will encounter obstacles, face moments of uncertainty, and struggle with self-doubt. But it is through these challenges that we learn, evolve, and become stronger.

The key to living a fulfilling life is not to chase perfection but to embrace progress. It is not to measure our worth by external accomplishments or validation, but by how closely our lives align with our authentic selves. When we live with purpose, we free ourselves from the pressures of comparison and create lives that are rich with meaning and fulfilment.

As you step forward into the future, know that you have the power to create the life you desire. You are enough, just as you are. The world needs your unique voice, your authenticity, and your purpose. Embrace your power, live with intention, and trust that the journey ahead is exactly where you are meant to be.

Your story is not defined by external expectations—it is defined by the choices you make, the values you live by, and the impact you have on the world around you. So step boldly into your future, with authenticity, humility, and a deep commitment to living a life that reflects your truest self.

www.ingramcontent.com/pod-product-compliance
Lightning Source LLC
LaVergne TN
LVHW021154160826
845679LV00024B/2116

* 9 7 9 8 8 9 6 3 2 7 6 9 1 *